Impact Investing in Africa

Edward Mungai

Impact Investing in Africa

A Guide to Sustainability for Investors, Institutions, and Entrepreneurs

Edward Mungai
Kenya Climate Innovation Center
Nairobi, Kenya

ISBN 978-3-030-00427-9   ISBN 978-3-030-00428-6 (eBook)
https://doi.org/10.1007/978-3-030-00428-6

Library of Congress Control Number: 2018958601

This Palgrave Macmillan imprint is published by the registered company Springer Nature Switzerland AG
The registered company address is: Gewerbestrasse 11, 6330 Cham, Switzerland

To my wife, Anne, and my children, Joan, Stacy, Anna-Lexxy and Jayden,
without whom this book would have been completed a year earlier.

Preface

'Africa rising,' 'the continent of the future,' and 'the next investment frontier' are all part of the narrative that we have heard for over ten years now as a way to describe what is happening to the African continent. Looking back, not much has been achieved, especially in solving the day-to-day problems that the inhabitants of the continent face. In no way am I saying that not much has been achieved; of course, more than 300 million people have been rescued from poverty in the last 15 or so years but more are still struggling in poverty. The point is that more needs to be done and the 'business as usual' approach will not solve the challenges. It has to be 'business *unusual*' and one such approach is through the shift from traditional investments and charity giving to a more deliberate way that combines both the traditional investments and charity in the form of impact investing or investing with a purpose.

This book demonstrates some of the ways through which financial returns can be generated whilst at the same time improving social and environmental conditions. Many of the people and institutions featured in this book have left their headquarters, cities and homes for the purpose of making money, but in a more meaningful way that benefits the communities. They believe that the best way to help is through meaningful investment and not through charity. I am writing this book in order to share my experiences with the reader about what is happening in the continent of Africa. The experiences, especially those of some investors, have not always been positive and, as indicated by some of the examples, money has been lost and impacts not achieved. In other cases, a great deal of money has been made but, more importantly, greater impacts in terms of money taxes to the exchequer, more jobs, increased availability of products to the bottom of the pyramid and so on have been achieved. The key is that I want to share this experience with the readers of this book and hopefully they will inspire action, namely to consider impact investing in Africa or to help shape the investment agenda in the continent.

As investment in new ventures across the African continent grows, and enterprises multiply in a wide variety of sectors, the next wave of challenges and opportunities has become apparent to those with the experience and vision to understand them. Identifying the trends, emerging sectors, and best political climates for impact investments requires personal, practical entrepreneurial experience; an international finance background; and a savvy understanding of how African business works. I hope that with my experience in the African continent, working with both the private sector and the public sector, will help me to offer some insights into these issues.

This is a book for investors, policymakers, entrepreneurs and everyone interested in the economic future of Africa. This book analyzes the current state of impact investments, and the best opportunities for the future. The book also notes that impact investment is expected to fuel explosive economic growth in a continent where the labor force is the fastest-expanding in the world, at a rate exceeding even China and India. It is projected to reach 2 billion people soon, and to surpass China and India by 2040. With increased access to labor, businesses of all sizes will enjoy greater ability to expand efficiently. Moreover, with increased access to jobs comes increased spending power for Africa's middle class. Africa's consumer markets are expected to increase in size dramatically in the coming decades. Indeed, the per capita income average for Africa is expected to reach the level of about US$4500 by 2030. As a result, the African Development Bank (AfDB) estimates that consumer spending in Africa will reach US$2.2 trillion by 2030.

This Is How the Book Will Unfold

Chapter 1 offers an introduction where I will define impact investing in the African context, using personal examples to show how the lives of ordinary people are being transformed through targeted investments. I will provide an outline of who is investing in these social enterprises—traditional private equity and asset management funds, development financial institutions (DFIs), foundations and family offices, banks and diversified financial institutions. In addition to looking at the state of impact investing in Africa, I will also make a case that the continent needs investment, not aid.

In Chapter 2, I will look at the business environment in Africa, stating what an entrepreneur and investors can expect to encounter as they set up business or invest in the continent. Africa is a dynamic market and there will always be challenges such as cost and time overruns, and a lack of proper enabling environments, among other challenges. In this chapter, I will provide some advice that will be useful in overcoming some of the challenges encountered investing or starting a business in Africa.

Chapter 3 is about how to scale impact investing and I explore in this chapter the ways in which an impact investor can align their impact targets with sustainable development goals, to ensure that they contribute to the economic growth and development of Africa. The sustainability of impact investments is also a key factor in the success of an impact investment.

Chapter 4 looks at the landscape of impacting investing in Africa where I provide the background of impact investing—the facts, numbers and the players—in Africa, and look at the key success factors that drive them. I provide a list of the hot spots for impact investing in Africa, singling out Kenya, Nigeria, Ghana, Rwanda and South Africa as examples where I show the different ways that foundations, pension funds and insurers, banks, sovereign wealth funds, multinationals, diaspora and retail investors are actively financing impact investments. I look at the different considerations that have defined the way the investors approach their investments, including financial returns, impact required, exit mechanisms and the risk appetite of the investor.

Chapter 5 is about the emerging trends in impact investing in Africa where I cast a forward glance at how the impact investing space in Africa is expected to evolve in the next few years. I provide key themes such as the rising importance of cross-border investments and how this will affect impact investing as well as future generations in the continent, among other trends.

Chapter 6 looks on how to structure an impact fund and I use the examples from my work at the Kenya Climate Innovation Center to illustrate how to structure an impact fund and some of the considerations in terms of the structure, strategies and core competencies that may be required. Key structures within a fund are critical, and I enumerate the need to have a solid board of advisors, an investment committee and a fund management team.

Chapter 7 looks at the question of measuring impact where I ask the question that is always on the table for an impact investor: How do we know that the investment is bringing about the intended change in the community? I provide different frameworks that can be used to measure the impact of the fund: the Logical Framework (LF), Results Framework (RF) and Performance Framework (PF). I also provide the principles that guide the measurement of impact, noting that this should be based on quantifiable evidence, should be participatory in order to include all stakeholders, and should be cost effective and clear. Measuring impact will help in building the case for future or additional investment.

Chapter 8 considers de-risking impact investments though the use of the Bright Chicks in Uganda case, a Danish-led investment that fell on hard times. I will consider some of the traits that an investor needs to have before tackling the African impact investing market, which can be fraught with risks at all stages of investment. Furthermore, I will provide ways of minimizing risk exposure that will call for proper performance reporting from the investee in order to catch problems early, proper selection of funding instruments, obtaining owner guarantees on the business and hand-holding the investee to transfer skills and improve their governance and management practices.

Finally, Chapter 9 will look into the challenges facing impact investing in Africa. Investors will always face challenges, especially when they are investing in a high-risk high-reward environment like sub-Saharan Africa. Some of these challenges are on the part of the investee, such as limited access to formal finance, lack of access to market information and facilities such as office space. On the part of the investor, there are a limited number of viable deals in Africa, making it more expensive to invest due to fierce competition. The investor also faces a problem when exiting an investment, with limited options for exiting due to underdeveloped capital markets. There are also problems within the investment ecosystem, with limited synergy between the different players and the enabling environment not always being up to scratch.

The vibrant growth of the African economy is being driven by a continent-wide entrepreneurial spirit. Even full-time employees frequently start and manage side businesses, and many of Africa's most successful new businesspeople are serial entrepreneurs. These are the people who should be encouraged to shift towards impact investing.

But which opportunities are real, and which are illusory? Which sectors are already beginning to mature, and which are poised to grow exponentially? This book explains in granular detail which sectors present the greatest opportunities for impact investors. The book examines a number of recent ventures across the content of Africa—both successes and failures—to explain and illustrate what will be likely to succeed in the near term.

Sectors such as financial services, telecommunications and agribusiness are increasingly growing and maturing in Africa, but they do carry some risk for investors who are less-familiar with the political, legal, social and geographical landscape. In the coming pages, I highlight some of these risks and opportunities as well as the ways to negotiate them.

Nairobi, Kenya
2018

Edward Mungai

Acknowledgements

It is evident that for this project to be successful it required many hands and brains to be involved. First, I would like to thank all the good people working in the impact sector; many of the concepts and strategies described in this book have emanated from the tireless work of these people. I have learnt a lot from each of you and am extremely grateful to you for sharing your insights and lessons with me. I thank you sincerely for your contributions to the impact sector; my work has only been possible through your dedication and labor. Thanks to my editors, Tula Weis and Joseph Johnson, from Palgrave Macmillan.

Specific mentions go to Marc J. Lane and Tim Brandhorst from The Law Offices of Marc J. Lane, P.C. in Chicago—thank you for your inspiration on this journey. To my friends Aun Ali Rahman and Masood Shariff from the World Bank, your insights, especially in regard to the fund formation and the work at Kenya Climate Ventures, helped to shape some of the pages within. Charles Mwaniki, Amos Gichinga, Henrik Anker-Ladefoged, Paul Ohaga and Sarah Kanaiya, your contributions and guidance made this book a possibility. To Carbon Trust team, led by David Aitken and Ian Cooke, your work was insightful to shaping this project.

I offer this book to all these people for their contributions to the value that I hope the book will create.

Contents

List of Figures

List of Tables

1

Introduction

In some ways, the challenges I faced thirty years ago growing up in a typical African village in central Kenya are the same ones children living there today continue to face: lack of electricity, poor nutrition, and inconsistent sanitation. Africa also continues to be, by far, the poorest continent; United Nations statistics show that two-thirds of the world's poorest countries are in Africa, where a full 40% of people live below the poverty line. For decades, governments and non-government institutions have struggled with these issues and have not had much success on the continent. Over the past ten years, however, people and governments have begun seeking change—through market-based solutions, and through the emergence of a triple-bottom-line framework that values social, environmental *and* financial dimensions.

A new class of entrepreneurs has arrived, working to provide solutions to the social and environmental challenges faced by the people of Africa. Innovations are happening in sectors such as agriculture, health, energy, education, water and sanitation, telecommunication, and finance and investments. These developments are fuelled in large part by an infusion of investment, not aid. Impact investing is the new way to do business in Africa, and it is proving to be the solution to deep-rooted problems that have flown under the radar of traditional donors and investors, governments and even local philanthropists.

Going back to my village, many people are paying the price for the realities we had to endure just to survive; painfully, my mother is one of them. She is partially blind! This happened in the last 10 years and the diagnosis has pointed at air pollution-related causes. The pollution that is to blame for

© The Author(s) 2018
E. Mungai, *Impact Investing in Africa*,
https://doi.org/10.1007/978-3-030-00428-6_1

her partial blindness is caused by the smoke that was perpetually to be found in her kitchen, where we cooked using all sorts of firewood.

In Africa, more than 80% of the population has been using wood fuels and paraffin as the primary source of household energy. A smokeless kitchen is a relatively new concept in the continent and, sadly, many of our women have already suffered the effects of smoke, even as they begin to shift to cleaner fuel.

Thankfully, we are seeing the increased emergence of entrepreneurs who are working to provide cleaner solutions such as biogas, clean cook stoves and alternative cooking fuels such as bioethanol. These entrepreneurs are not just making money in a space that was previously unexploited, but they are also making sure that future generations will not pay the same price as many women like my mother who spent years in smoky kitchens.

The common thread to all the challenges noted above is the low level of disposable income among many of those living in African countries. Millions in this age still live on less than a dollar per day, which means that they cannot access many of the utilities and services that those with money come to take for granted.

What Is Impact Investing, and Why Is It Now Showing Growth?

Impact investing is not philanthropy. It is business that addresses the challenges that humankind faces and offers a reasonable return to the financiers of the business. Multiple factors have aligned to bring about this change. I have seen first-hand the increased economic activity and developments in more than thirty African countries. There have been marked improvement in the state of the roads, the size of the markets, and infrastructure growth has set the stage for significant gains in commerce; while the continent's economy overall is growing at an average rate of 5%, many countries predict double-digit growth rates.

Africa has the fastest-expanding labor force in the world—and will surpass that of China and India by the year 2040. This workforce is young: over 60% of the population is under the age of 25 years.[1] And increasingly, it is urban. More than 40% of Africans live in cities, with some countries such as Angola, Ghana, and Nigeria boasting over 80% urbanization levels.

---

[1]*Africa: Tapping into Growth Opportunities, Challenges and Strategies for Consumer Products*. Deloitte.

Thus, both the labor market and the resulting expanded markets for goods and services are increasingly concentrated, making business growth easier and cheaper.

The population growth of the continent and that fact that it is the youngest continent currently and in the near future is a great potential for businesses. It is estimated that by 2050 the continent will be home to over 2.5 billion people and half of this population will be under the age of 25 years.[2]

This, on one hand, presents an opportunity and on the other hand a challenge. The challenge is whether the continent will have the capacity to maintain the population growth in a sustainable way. Impact investing, which will bring the needs of all the stakeholders together, seems like the solution that will help move the continent towards sustainability despite the huge population growth.

This progress has resulted in a middle class who now account for over 30% of the African population. The Economic Intelligence Unit (EIU) forecasts that by 2030, the continent's top 18 cities could have a combined spending power of US$1.3 trillion.[3]

Consumers in the rapidly growing middle class have also become more sophisticated regarding new products and services, frontiers that were non-existent fifteen years ago. Mobile telecommunication is transforming the way Africa does business, with over 600 million subscribers in 2017.[4] Kenya alone, with over 30 million subscribers, has more phone users today compared with the whole of African continent fifteen years ago. The middle-class category is rising and will be the main driver of the consumer demand in the continent.

Another factor that is contributing to the growth in the continent is the stability in government and government policies compared to twenty to thirty years ago. Governments are now more progressive and are working toward improving the welfare of Africans. Many now offer an enabling environment for business, improving infrastructure and ensuring the right economic and regulatory environment to attract Foreign Direct Investment (FDI).

---

[2]United Nations, Department of Economic and Social Affairs, Population Division. 2015. *World Population Prospects: The 2015 Revision, Key Findings and Advance Tables*. Working Paper No. ESA/P/WP.241.

[3]*Africa: Open for Business. The Potential, Challenges and Risks*. A Report from the Economist Intelligence Unit.

[4]GSMA.

The main target of FDI is industrial development that benefits locals through the creation of jobs and the provision of social services.

There are some small patches where political change has not yet happened, but it is just a matter of time before we start seeing change. The political shifts that happened in 2018 in South Africa, Ethiopia and Zimbabwe are just an example of what to expect in the future. These changes are good for business and will be expected to result to more impact investing activities in the continent. However, it is not enough for businesses to just generate revenues, they must also solve some of the challenges faced by Africans if they are to be sustainable in the long term.

This policy of lifting others up as part of the process of growth creates a sustainable economy, which will open up further opportunities not just for individual business but also spawn auxiliary entrepreneurs.

For a continent with societies that are often fraught with conflict and fraction, building a sustainable economy that is inclusive of all goes a long way towards fostering peace.

For social enterprises to thrive, they will need capital. The type of capital required for this is high-risk capital and capital that is not only looking for the financial returns but also looking for social returns. Impact investing in enterprises that seek more than just profit can solve the problem above, but it does call for a different kind of investor. Unfortunately, there are not many who are willing to invest in such businesses due to their size (i.e., small) as well as the level of expected financial return (i.e., minimal).

Those of us who have seen the benefit of impact investing therefore are obliged to spread its gospel and educate our people and investors on the sustainability of enterprise that improves the lives of people (who are also future customers, once they leave the poverty trap). In this book, I will endeavour to show that impact investing is the new way to do business, using examples of impactful investing that I have seen across the African continent in the course of over 20 years of working for the private sector, public sector and non-profit sector for global institutions.

Who Are the Current Impact Investors and What Have They Put in So Far?

Institutional impact investors have noted the potential that the African continent presents in terms of the possibility for pipeline companies as well as the impacts that that they can have. These investors have embraced these developments and created funds accordingly.

A 2017 survey conducted by the Global Impact Investing Network (GIIN)[5] reported US$114 billion of impact funds are in assets under management. In 2017, sub-Saharan Africa was the beneficiary of over 10% of the total funds under management for impact investing, which made it the second-highest allocation of the resources related to impact investing globally, after Canada and the USA, which had 40% of the funds under management.

Impact investment financing comes from a variety of sources, including the traditional private equity and asset management funds, development financial institutions (DFIs), foundations and family offices, banks and diversified financial institutions, as well as other institutional investors. In the recent past, we have also seen crowd-funded financing coming into play. This will include companies such as KIVA, which are crowdsourcing finance in order to invest in impact businesses.

In the recent past, and with the growth of impact investing, there has been a shift in way business and interventions to eradicate poverty are being approached. This is because the impact investing route leads to interventions that are market-based and that are more sustainable compared with the old way of doing things, which was to provide grants to resolve the challenges faced by the continent. This is the way forward for the continent: a shift from 'help' with financing to partnerships through impact investments. This follows the old adage that advocates showing a man how to fish rather than simply giving him the fish if one is truly interested in the sustainability of the project.

Impact investing has provided the opportunity for private and public financing to focus not only on the financial returns but also on social and environmental needs based on a market-based approach. However, we are still in the early days. More financial flows as well as innovative financing mechanisms to help in resolving the continent challenges are expected as more and more impact investors and impact related entrepreneurs thrive in the continent.

The expectations are that the financiers will be able to make financial returns as well as cause impacts in the continent in the forms of jobs, more disposable incomes in the pockets of the African population, better safeguarding of the environment, positively influence social issues and provide services that otherwise would not have been possible.

---

[5]2017 Annual Impact Investor Survey.

In the last ten or so years, impact investing has become a focal point for foundations, non-governmental organisations (NGOs) and high-net-worth individuals (HNWIs). This has resulted in a number of participants in the sector who are aiming to provide financing in order to impact related businesses.

On the other hand, there has been a significant growth in the number of people willing to start businesses, which should help in resolving the challenges that our world—especially Africa—is facing, making social entrepreneurship more attractive.

College students, recent graduates, serial entrepreneurs, wealthy business people, foundations, commercial investment vehicles and even big commercial banks, among others, have discovered impact investments as a viable asset class, especially due to the potential for impact and the stories associated with the sector.

In the recent past, Danish pensioners, as an example, have been pushing their fund managers to look into the African continent and to make meaningful investments with their pension funds. This has resulted in more Danish pensions fund looking into the areas of climate finance, agriculture finance and micro finance with the hope that these will create more meaningful returns, as requested by their major stakeholder—the pensioners.

To fulfil the need for investable businesses in the continent, entrepreneurs and existing business are working on overdrive mode to come up with start-ups that will resolve the challenge as well as attracting the available finance to make their dreams come true. It may be said that the continent is experiencing a start-up fever. This is a repeat of what was experienced in other developing countries such as India, Brazil, Malaysia and China. This fever can be likened to the start-up fever that previously emerged in the USA in San Francisco, Austin and Seattle, which has spawned global corporate giants such as Facebook, Google and Amazon.

Start-up ecosystems are emerging in Nairobi, Lagos and Pretoria, all with the aim of producing businesses that will provide goods and services to the people of the continent.

The development progress in Africa seen in the last decade has been achieved due to the mix of interventions from various players such as governments, development partners, multilateral organizations such as the World Bank and IMF, the private sector, civil society and academia; these stakeholders have worked relentlessly to make the African continent a better place.

This enabling environment has worked as an enabler for the impact investment sector. There is still more to be done in order to achieve the full potential of the sector and this will be highlighted in the chapter discussing the challenges of impact investing in Africa.

Investment, Not Aid

Historically, development aid was the main way that development partners attempted to spur on economic development. In some instances, this has worked and in others it has been a disaster.

We have 50 years' experience and counting of failed development on the African continent. In that time, trillions of US dollars in the form of aid from the West has been deployed to the continent and it has failed to put the Sub-Saharan Africa out of poverty.

The developed world was, for a long time, fixated on the idea that plain vanilla aid was the solution to the challenges of the African continent, but this is now a thing of the past. Africa requires innovative development financing in the form of delivery mechanisms and structuring, as well the instruments for delivering these funds.

Investment in the private sector and in infrastructure projects must take centre stage in the African development narrative. This is not to say that there will be no need for aid in the continent—there will certainly be need for aid—but the caveat is that the old way of providing aid is not effective and development partners must aim to become more innovative in terms of how to provide aid. In the past, for instance, locals were not involved in determining the nature of financing; how much was needed as well as the financing instruments, which has resulted to disaster in terms of the effectiveness of the aid provided.

Indeed, the trend over the next 10 or so years will be that of moving from aid to trade, which will mean that the developed nations will be looking into mechanisms that can lead to trading in the developing countries and hence present a win–win situation for both sides of the divide. We have already seen this in practice with The Netherlands, which recently said that it will stop issuing Kenya with aid assistance, and instead will engage with the country as a trade partner going forward. It is instructive that the Netherlands has already become Kenya's second biggest export destination, buying goods worth US$500 million in 2017.[6] This is the way forward for Africa's development partners if the continent is to be lifted from chronic dependence on handouts.

---

[6]Worlds Top Exports, 2017.

Looking back, in the twentieth century, some of the best interventions by the developed nations in Africa involve cases where real investments as opposed to grants have taken the centre stage, including the works carried out by the DFIs in Africa with investments in agribusiness, infrastructure, and manufacturing and service industries, resulting in millions of jobs. These projects generated billions of US dollars paid as taxes to governments for the provisions of public goods.

Private sector investments should chase returns since they are readily available in Africa but more importantly there is need to share value with all the stakeholders involved in such investment including the government of the day through taxes paid as well as the host communities. The new trajectory will also result in multiplier effects as the interventions will have long-standing benefits for the economies in Africa.

What Is the Best Possible Solution for Africa?

Private sector and market-driven interventions will definitely play a key role in the economic development of the African continent. Traditional private sector intervention has played a significant role in development in Africa, especially where business models allow for benefit sharing with other stakeholders. However, the situation is complicated when it comes to the provision of social or public good. In most instances, citizens and the private sector have expected social or public good to be provided by the government. Unfortunately, this has not been the case, due to limited resources.

To bridge the gap, the emergence of social/mission-driven enterprises has been on the rise and these have a huge potential in moving developing countries towards development and, at the same time, in solving the challenges faced by such developing countries.

There has been a huge global movement toward impact investing, which is giving rise to social enterprises aimed at solving the challenges on a market-based approach that will have needed the government to resolve. Impact investing in Africa remains nascent and has the potential to resolve the African challenges especially in health, education, social services, provision of energy and so on, and at the same time contribute to the continent's economic growth and development objectives.

As noted above, in the past, the African continent was focused on official development assistance (ODA) from developed and other emerging markets, in order to meet the basic service needs of their populations. Due to the uncertainty faced by the global economies, it is expected that ODA will no longer be the major source of development financing in developing countries.

Private sources of capital will play a larger role, where it will be used to improve access to social services in Africa. In other ways, as noted above, ODA will be more innovative and will be driven by the market-based approach, which will be more efficient and effective.

In the last decade, there has been a significant increase in the private financial flows to Africa, as traditional ODA declines. This will mean that there is a need for the African governments to provide the relevant space to attract even more private funding, especially where those funds will be able to provide for public goods in a market-based approach.

This will, in turn, be of help in addressing the socio-economic challenges by providing market-based solutions that address the priority areas such as health, education, water and energy supplies, among others. Impact investment has the potential to meet the needs of these priority areas and to complement public spending and ODA. This will be achieved by bringing in private sector capital and skills to reduce African economies' vulnerability to external shocks, providing a market-based solution to address socio-economic needs.

In some instances, there will be need for allowing ODA and other public funds to focus on addressing social needs for which there is currently no viable market-based solution.

In other words, the need for ODA has not completely vanished, but rather it will become more innovative and the cases in which it is carried out on a non-market basis will become fewer and fewer.

Conclusion

Now and in the future, Africa—long dependent on aid—will instead rely on investment to fuel its growth. Rapid growth is expected, because of the rise of the middle class, stable governments, urbanization and improved infrastructure.

Both large-scale institutional opportunities and smaller-scale opportunities for direct investment will be prevalent in the future—and the remainder of this book will describe the most attractive options available to investors as well as the remaining challenges.

Our focus is on impact investing, which we view as a solution to the semi stand-off between development aid financing and bank financing of ventures and enterprises in Africa.

We will look at the state of impact investing in Africa, the challenges businesses are facing in this kind of venture and how to structure and manage funds. We will also explore emerging trends that will inform the transformation of impact investing in the next decade.

2

Doing Business in Africa: What to Consider

Africa is the youngest continent in the world in terms of the age of its population. This situation will persist considering that the population growth rates in Africa are on the rise. For the past 10 years or so, the continent has experienced high population growth as well as an impressive and sustained economic growth and sustainable development.

Child mortality has dropped, and the number of children born per woman has been on the rise. Depending on how this is viewed, it may be seen as an opportunity for economic growth since it will represent an asset to the continent, both in terms of the provision of a labor force in the future as well as a market for products and services, and hence it will contribute to the economic growth of the continent.

The growth in the population is attributed to various factors such as the fact that African men want big families to enhance their status in society. This is in contrast to what their counterparts in the Western world believe. Many African men have families with over three children, which has a big effect on the population of the continent.

The life expectancy in Africa according to the World Health Organization (WHO) is 60 years for females and 57 years for males. The adult mortality rates as of the last official statistics by WHO in 2016 was at 281 per 1000 for females and 332 per 1000 for males.[1]

Improvement of education in Africa has been top of the African agenda since it is part of the global agenda. Africa was not able to fully achieve the

---

[1]United Nations Population Division. *World Population Prospects: 2017 Revision.*

© The Author(s) 2018
E. Mungai, *Impact Investing in Africa*,
https://doi.org/10.1007/978-3-030-00428-6_2

Millennium Development Goals (MDG) goals with regard to access to basic education even though there was significance progress in various regions in Africa, with Kenya and Rwanda among the countries that recorded commendable milestones in terms of access to basic education, despite the challenges that they face in ensuring that basic education is accessible to all.

These demographic trends are forming important drivers of economic growth in Africa. There is a need to take advantage of this economic growth in order to deliver better livelihoods for the population across the continent.

Over the next 20 years, these trends are projected to lead to even higher levels of economic growth throughout Africa. However, these gains will be subject to the strategies and policies that will be put in place, especially by the governments of the countries in Africa.

Unfortunately, there will be no standard polices and strategies for the whole of Africa since the continent is made up of 54 countries and hence the intervention will be as many as the number of the countries in the continent.

The policy frameworks adapted by the countries will have an impact on demographic trends and should focus on development goals. It will also be important for these frameworks to consider Agenda 2030, which will be achieved through the Sustainable Development Goals (SDGs) as endorsed in September 2015 by United Nations in New York. The key areas to focus on are poverty reduction, food sufficiency, education, health, security and the provision of public services.

The competitive advantage provided by the young demographic will most likely provide an opportunity to increase the average disposable income, which in turn will reduce the poverty levels as well as yielding other demographic dividends that will lead to economic success of the African continent.

If well executed, the interventions will help Africa to move along the same trajectory as the Asian emerging markets where as much as one-third of economic growth was mapped to demographic change in Asia. There is also a risk that the growth in population will be a risk to development, especially if the right policies are not put in place.

Africa is the second largest continent, both in population and land mass, with a population of over 1.2 billion people in 2017 and on over 30 million square kilometres of land. It is the home of over 15% of the global population. More than two-thirds of the population live on farms or in small villages—a fact that is changing at a very fast rate due to rural–urban migration.

The continent is divided into 54 states, all of which except Morocco are members of the African Union. The mention of Africa elicits ideas of abject poverty, a source of slaves in the medieval times, corruption and political chaos. It is also known for its sportive population, safaris, abundant natural resources, great weather, rich cultural heritage, as well as being the home of some of the world's most popular geographical features, such as deserts, mountains, and rich flora and fauna.

In Africa, over 1500 languages are spoken, which makes Africa the home of one in four of every language spoken on globe. World civilization started in Africa and specifically in Egypt, which was an existent state in 3300 BC and formed the oldest literate civilization.

The good African weather is not by chance but rather is a result of the continent being the most centrally placed on the globe with both the 0-degree longitude and 0-degree latitude cutting across the continent. The African continent is divided into two; sub-Saharan Africa and North Africa. All countries that are located south of the Sahara Desert are part of sub-Saharan- Africa—which is most of the African countries. North Africa, on the other hand, forms the states north of the Sahara, mainly Arab states that are also part of the Arab League. Somalis, Comoros and Djibouti, despite being on the south of the Sahara, are part of the Arab league.

The whole of Africa was colonized by the Europeans, with the exception of two countries, Ethiopia and Liberia. Most of the African countries received their independence in the 1960s, making them over 50 years old. The colonization of the African states is very evident wherever you travel across Africa, because hangovers of colonization still exist. From tea drinking in Kenya, which was influenced by the British, to the port wine in Mozambique, borrowed from the Portuguese, the hangovers are many.

Africa has enjoyed several benefits from colonization, such as the introduction of formal education, improvement of the healthcare systems, the realization of the women's rights and the continued benefit of the tourism industry among others.

There have been significant shortcomings as well as benefits from the effect of colonization and it is very difficult to say with authority whether it was a good or bad thing that the African continent was taken over in the 1800s.

For instance, foreign languages are spoken in Africa, with French being spoken by more people in African than in France. English is the language for most of the countries in Africa, which signifies the presence of British rule in the continent.

Religion is another import that was delivered from colonization, in addition to the crops that were brought to Africa from Europe such as coffee and tea among other products.

Fast forward to the present day, Africa is a hot-bed of internet growth with 28.7% internet penetration according to the internet world statistics. Internet users in Africa are at 9.3% of global internet users. Most of the access to the Internet is through mobile phone devices as computers are still not affordable to most Africans. In Africa, more than 50% of the population do not have mobile phones. This is due to affordability; more than 40% of Africans still live on less than US$2 a day.

The technology boom cannot go unnoticed and innovations driven by the mobile phone and internet connectivity are happening in Africa left, right and centre. This has resulted in the emergence of some of the world's most innovative ideas, such as mobile money transfers, M-Kopa Solar and other related innovations across the continent. In the 1990s and early 2000s, the landline as well as mobile phone were for an exclusive club of people who were viewed as rich.

With liberalization, which in-turn created an enabling environment, the industry has witnessed huge positive changes that have empowered Africans.

Fifty years since independence, the African continent is still struggling with abject poverty, low infrastructure development, low disposable incomes, poor heath, low literacy levels, a lack of electricity connectivity and a lack of financial inclusiveness, among other challenges.

In the recent past, the narrative for Africa has been 'Africa rising' with the continent experiencing economic growth, an emerging market boom, rapid urbanization and a growing middle class that is expected to lead to a rise in the demand for goods and services, which in turn will lead to economic growth in the continent. However, this does not apply to the entire African continent as some of the countries are still struggling in terms of development.

Africa is characterized by vast inequalities in income and wealth distribution that have undermined development. In most instances, development appears to be within the 50 km radius from the capitals, which raises the question of inclusivity and the distribution of wealth as the continent develops. Rural–urban migration in Africa has been very rapid, leading to a net expansion of informal settlements with countries such as Angola, Kenya, South Africa, Egypt and Ghana having slums that are in a very bad state. The informal settlements that are predominantly found in large cities are a clear illustration of wealth and income inequality in Africa.

Both the public and the private sectors have a collective role in equitable development and this should not be looked at solely as the role of either sector, but rather as a role in which the two sectors have to collaborate. The challenge with this perspective is that there must be a definite business case in order for the private sector to engage in equitable development. So far, the business case has not been built specifically for mainstream businesses, which have traditionally focused on a single bottom line of profit.

Movements toward triple bottom line, mission-driven and impact investment in Africa are good ways to move the private sector towards participating in Africa's sustainable development. This will have definite value for the shareholders as it has now been proven that doing good by taking care of the social and environmental aspects of the business, is also good business for the private sector.

The World Bank report on Ease of Doing Business[2] shows that sub-Saharan African countries have an average ranking of 143. In the ease of doing business rankings prepared by the World Bank, countries are ranked according to how easy it is to start a business, get permits, pay taxes, trade across borders, enforce contracts and register property.

African countries have generally improved over the past decade, but most still populate the lower end of the rankings out of a global count of 190 economies. This tells us that doing business on the African continent is not an easy thing, and in some areas, it is not for the faint-hearted. Amazingly though, this represents an improvement on previous years, although much still needs to be done.

For instance, in 2017, more than 30 countries in Africa implemented reforms that would make them become a more attractive investment destination. These reforms included improvements the in business registration process, land investment and transfer reform, and improvements in access to credit, making it easier to do business.

According to the World Bank's Doing Business report, 2017 Africa had the largest number of reforms than any other region to date. Malawi, Nigeria and Zambia were among the most improved countries.

The notion of attracting investment by making it easier to do business for outsiders in a country is taking root in Africa, replacing the previous approach, which saw nations make it difficult for foreigners to set up a business in the name of protecting local businesses. Shining examples of this change include Rwanda, Ghana and Botswana, and to some extent Kenya— these countries have reduced the time it takes for a foreigner to licence a business and have cut down on the myriad of licences and permits needed to conduct business.

---

[2]World Bank. 2018. *Doing Business 2018: Reforming to Create Jobs.* Washington, DC: World Bank. https://doi.org/10.1596/978-1-4648-1146-3. License: Creative Commons Attribution CC BY 3.0 IGO.

We have also seen the liberalization of capital flows, with the removal of the many restrictions on the movement of foreign exchange across borders, which previously made investors wary of African economies. However, the flip side is that you will still face some of the old problems that made the continent a daunting frontier for the wary investors.

Corruption is often flagged as the biggest problem for an investor in Africa, and for those investing across borders, regulations often differ even within the same geographical and economic bloc. There has been a movement by many counties in the continent to regionalize and decentralize governance, which to some extent will mean different regulations within a given country. Investors need to be wary of the changes happening and keep up to date with the changes and what these changes mean for investments.

An investor therefore needs to know a few things about doing business in Africa, which is a different animal from Western world of business, or even business in South America and Asia.

I will go through a few of the dos and don'ts of doing business on the continent based on experiences I have seen in various countries, but the reader should keep in mind that each country presents its own unique opportunities and challenges for a business person. This advice is more for those who are looking into investing in the continent as well as those who are designing innovative funds flow models' for the purposes of moving the African continent out of poverty.

Budget for Time and Cost Overruns

Africa is a dynamic market and there are a lot of factors that will result in cost and time overruns. Things tend to move a little slower on the continent, where there is considerable red tape to be negotiated. Generally, projects will require more money than initially thought and take longer to implement. It is therefore important for any manager to account for such unforeseeable overruns.

Normally, I would recommend for 25% of the budget to be set aside in the project costs to cover for such overruns. This will mean that the funds need to set aside some dry powder for further investment in the transactions. The truth of the matter is that I have seen investments collapsing and investors exiting with half-completed projects due to cost overruns. One strategy will always be to have a deep-pocket investor as part of the investment consortium who will be able to protect the other investors just in case there are cost overruns.

One painful truth about many African countries is that you may face demands for 'on-the-side' payments to oil the gears of officialdom when setting up a business. This is where the issue of time overrun, which in most cases will be lead to cost overrun, comes in to the play.

I would not recommend bribery, since the receiver will keep coming back for more and hence this approach will not be sustainable. It is not the way to do business; it is cheating and cheating in this sector never pays. It is better to do no business at all than to be involved in a dirty deal, especially for an impact investor who is looking to make meaningful change while earning a return from an enterprise.

To mitigate the risk, investors should ensure that they have a proper governance system and that they have implemented a control environment that will have processes and procedures for ensuring that cost and time overruns are identified and addressed as early as possible.

The governance system should also be able to propose ways for how to deal with such overruns when they occur. Investors should put more resources and efforts into the due diligence and planning phase in order to ensure that investments are kept in check though the investment cycle. This will include having proper planning and implementation systems and tools that will ensure robust work plans and budgets for the investments and at the same time carrying out a detailed risk analysis for the investments.

As an example of this, I was involved in hotel projects in Kenya and Ethiopia that aimed to have Scandinavian hotel brands managing the hotels. These projects had different investors, some of whom had deep pockets. Honestly, were it not for the deep-pocketed investors such as Development Financial Institutions (DFIs), these two investments could not have progressed.

It is important to note that both projects had over 50% cost and time overruns, which raised questions with regard to the fundamentals of the investments and how long they will take to result in financial returns, as this was key in addition to the impacts returns from the projects.

Value Chain Considerations

It is important to think through the full value chain requirements of your project—often the suppliers and business partners are not there and it is necessary to ensure that before you kick off your project, all the value chain participants (various suppliers) are in place. It is not uncommon to find out that you have set up a factory only to realise that one of the suppliers of a necessary component is not available. Therefore, it is important to get all the elements of your business in line before setting up. Due diligence before investment is doubly important in Africa, where factors such as availability of transport and logistics links, raw materials availability, customer mapping and competitors and so on can make or break a business.

A recent report by consultancy firm McKinsey & Company on Chinese investments in Africa[3] showed that these Chinese firms are forced to source up to 53% of their supplies from their mother country, because African suppliers simply cannot provide the volumes and quality of supplies needed, especially by manufacturing firms. It is therefore prudent to identify needs and to seek out trustworthy suppliers. This can be done by setting up links with established businesses that have previously done business on the continent and seeking out their suppliers. In Africa, business relationships matter, and a good network is almost critical for a business to survive.

Value chain consideration will also provide a possibility for better opportunities for the investors. In most cases, the investors who had the plan to invest in one section of the value chain going beyond that stage and integrating either backward or forward in most cases to unlock more value for their investments.

It is therefore critical that an investor looks at the investment from a value chain perspective. For example in 2010, I was involved in a proposed pig farm investment in Tanzania. The main promoter of the investment was a Danish investor who was looking at setting up a piggery near Dar es Salaam with the aim of reaching about 750 sows at full capacity. This was to be the biggest pig farm in Tanzania. At the due diligence stage, indications were that there were no proper feed mills in Tanzania and the uptake of the pork would not be sustainable at the levels suggested.

This called for the investor to think about integrating forward and backwards—forward by having a slaughter house, packing operations and marketing operations and backwards by having an investment in the feed mills. This is how consideration for the value chain should help to develop the proposed investment as well as making more value and mitigating the risks involved as well as providing the opportunity for additional investment and the resulting impacts. In this case, there were more jobs that were created than had been expected as well as other social and environmental impacts as a result of the expansion of the investment concept and possibilities.

---

[3]Dance of the lions and dragons June 2017; How are Africa and China engaging, and how will the partnership evolve?

Pay Attention to Legal Issues

It is critical that any investor in Africa should consider all the legal issues relating to the business or the investment in question. There are a number of legal issues that will have an influence on investors in Africa, including those that are common to investments in most international ventures, such as company structures, taxation, competition law and employment aspects.

More recent developments in the areas of corporate governance, anti-money laundering and environmental law have been introduced in Africa and should be considered by any investor interested in Africa. It is recommended that before an investment, a legal due diligence be carried out to ensure that all the legal issues are addressed before an investor commits money to projects. Normally, this will be in the form of a legal opinion from a reputable legal firm. There are many legal firms and investors need to undertake due diligence to determine which are the best legal firms to provide opinions and advice.

Of course, this should be at the Investment management firm costs and will also vary from firm to firm across Africa. There may be need for the investments firms to ask for professional indemnity from the partners of the firm to make sure that they are safeguarded just in case the advice provided is faulty. Once the investment is made, the investee companies and the investors must keep track of the laws and regulations. This is because many of these laws are still being developed and it is therefore easy for a business to fall foul of the law if it does not keep up with the latest amendments.

Some African governments are also very sensitive about the dealings of foreigners on their soil, and laws are sometimes enforced with undue enthusiasm or strictness. For the long-term success of your business, it is important to keep within the law.

Fortunately, there are a number of international and local law firms across Africa that have very good legal experts on African business laws and that can provide expert advice for a new business.

While making investments, it makes sense to have arbitration as part of dispute resolution since the legal process in Africa can take a lot of time. It is therefore important to ensure that arbitration clauses are included in the legal agreements for investment. A case in point here is the investment in Bright Chicks Uganda, which is discussed later in this book. In this case the investor fell out with his local partner and the case took over 10 years to be determined. Unfortunately, the law is that if there are any pending cases in a given investment, investors and implementers of the project should be halted until the case is determined. This can result to massive losses on the investor's side and many investments have been lost in this way. Arbitration could be a solution to this challenge.

Maintain a Strong Work Ethic

Today's business environment is a competitive one and companies that do not focus on good ethical policy are likely to find themselves in financial trouble in the long term. This is very relevant in Africa and in order to succeed, it is imperative to ensure that all those involved in the business are of high ethical standards.

When investors act with strong moral conduct they establish a great reputation for themselves, which also reflects on their companies as well. Once a person becomes known as someone who is ethical, people will want to do business or to work with them. Acting with strong moral fibre establishes trust and credibility with other investors, suppliers, colleagues, and customers, which in turn is of benefit to the business.

Be Flexible, Except with Core Values

It is a given that your plans and strategies will change as time goes on. There is a need to be flexible to changes. Investors should be aware that plans keep on changing in Africa and it is necessary for investors to accommodate those changes.

However, it is important that no matter the pressure for immediate impacts and profits, as well as other requirements, that investors do not compromise on the core values of the business. Some of the foreign businesses that are counted as the most successful in Africa only became a success after they 'Africanized.'

As is the case anywhere in the world, the quick way to become a success is to adopt local practices so that locals can consider you one of their own. A good example is the Kenyan mobile telecommunications sector, where one company, Safaricom, has become the undisputed market leader because locals have come to view it as 'their' company, as opposed to competitors who are seen as 'foreign firms.'

No one remembers that Safaricom is majority-owned by the British firm Vodafone. The firm's name is a starting point, with Kenyans identifying with the Safari in Safaricom, perhaps more than they would with names such as

Airtel, Celtel, Zain, Orange and any other of the various names adopted by competitors over the years. It may seem trivial, but it matters. Safaricom has also labelled all its promotions, services and products in Swahili, giving them a local flavour and identity, which has resonated with Kenyans. Yet in all of this, the company has maintained core values that are not dissimilar with those of the mother company in the UK. This shows that it is possible to be flexible to fit in with the locals whilst also maintaining high standards.

It is important to keep an eye on geopolitical matters for cross-border business. When conducting business across borders, it is vital to be aware of the fact that in Africa there is rarely any uniformity in business conditions such as you would likely find in Europe or parts of Asia.

Let us use the East Africa regions as an example. A business may be head-quartered in Nairobi, Kenya, with units spread across the region in countries such as Uganda, Tanzania, South Sudan and Rwanda. The conflict in South Sudan means that the movement and safety of workers there would be compromised, whilst there is no such problem in the other countries. At the same time, it may be easy to move capital and supplies across the borders of Uganda, Kenya and Rwanda, but difficult to do so across to Tanzania. This will have impact on the success of the investments and as I noted above, may call for looking at the value chains in the respective countries for better performance of the investment.

Paying Taxes

Tax laws can differ greatly across Africa, even where countries subscribe to the same economic bloc. For instance, in East Africa, the value added tax (VAT) for Kenya is 16%, compared with 18% in Uganda, Rwanda and Tanzania. As an investor, this variance will be seen on your cost of setting up, the cost of supplies and final cost of your goods or services in different countries. The same applies to other taxes such as excise, customs and even income tax for your labor force. It is therefore prudent to employ the services of a knowledgeable, trustworthy tax advisor to guide you through the many taxes in a country before you invest.

Information on these taxes can sometimes be hard to come by, even for the best resourced investor, since most countries have not taken their tax systems online. However, a few countries have made good strides in reforming their tax systems, implementing online platforms for the filing and payments of taxes and other levies due from an investor. By the beginning of 2018, economies including Kenya, Zambia, Rwanda, Mauritania, Angola,

Senegal, Togo and Botswana are implementing or have implemented systems to allow their citizens file and pay taxes online.

Closing Thoughts

As we have seen, running a business in Africa is not an open and shut case. It is a lot more complex than one would find, say, in Europe or North America.

As a business that is trying to impact positively the lives of people, it helps to be aware of the policy and social pitfalls that can befall your business, and to try to navigate them as early as possible, so that your goals can be met. We have noted that the continent is still struggling with abject poverty, low infrastructure development, low income, poor heath, low literacy levels, and a lack of electricity connectivity and financial inclusiveness.

These are the problems you will be trying to address through your impact investments, and at the same time make a return on your outlay. It must be said that it is a difficult thing to make money in a situation such as the one described above. However, things are changing, and that is the point we have emphasized here as we try to look at opportunities for impact investors in Africa.

The African continent is experiencing economic growth, an emerging market boom, rapid urbanization and a growing middle class that is expected to lead to a rise in the demand for goods and services, leading to economic growth in the continent.

As we shall see in later chapters, failure by foreign investors to do proper due diligence and to adapt to their new environment can have disastrous consequences at the end, breaking down a good idea into failure. Even as you take advantage of this new wind of change in Africa, a few key pointers to remember are as follows.

Policy frameworks adapted by countries will have an impact, and they do differ between countries. If you will do business across borders, arm yourself with enough advice on how to negotiate the different jurisdictions. This applies to both the laws of setting up a business and tax regulations.

Corruption is also one of the biggest problems facing businesses in Africa, and it is important to remain vigilant in order to avoid being on receiving end of corrupt individuals. My advice is to steer clear from using bribery to get things done.

We have also seen that most times, projects will require more money than initially thought and take longer to implement. Africa is full of nascent, greenfield opportunities in industries that were not existent on her soil before. While these areas provide investors with a fantastic opportunity to make money and to have a meaningful impact on people, they come with a lot of unseen challenges and costs that must be taken into account.

Therefore, it is important to get all the elements of your business in line before setting up, and prepare to be asked to be more innovative and flexible than you would be if you were investing in the developed world. With this in mind, you should be in a better position to meet the challenges and take advantage of the opportunities that come with impact investing in Africa. In the next chapter, we shall look at how your investments will scale down to the community you are trying to impact.

3

How Does Impact Investing Scale Down to Ordinary People?

In March 2013, a young Kenyan graduate, Peter Chege, knocked on the door at Kenya Climate Innovation Center (KCIC) with an idea for how to help Kenyan dairy farmers make animal fodder that would increase their yields significantly as well as save more than 70% in water usage.

The technology behind Peter's innovation was the use of a hydroponic system for small-scale farmers in Kenyan Highlands. The system that he was proposing is less sophisticated compared with similar ones in the Western world.

From first mention, the technology seemed mundane, but a closer look revealed an innovation that would aid the fight against climate change as well as increase the disposable income among the small-scale farmers.

Peter was looking at how the Centre could help him to improve his business through the business advisory services provided by KCIC, help in prototyping and piloting his idea; fundraising for scaling the business as well as helping in the accessing to market for his products to farmers.

Three years down the line, the business has come along in leaps and bounds, serving a total of over 2500 farmers in East Africa. In addition, the business has expanded to include the development of hydroponic systems for vegetables, and Peter's company is now the proud employer of over 35 full-time staff and has indirectly created another 130 jobs. This case is a good illustration of how impact investing can contribute to development in Africa.

The business above is currently in the market for impact investors to participate in its expansion.

© The Author(s) 2018
E. Mungai, *Impact Investing in Africa*,
https://doi.org/10.1007/978-3-030-00428-6_3

Kenya Climate Ventures, a fund that I helped to establish and that is currently 100% owned by KCIC, has invested US$300,000 in a convertible debt in the company and continues to provide technical assistance to the company.

Africa, and specifically the Sub-Saharan Africa region, is expected to attract more than 15% of the total global impact assets under management over the next five years. This financing will definitely enable the required changes and hence will move the continent to the next level in terms of development.

The expectations are that the financiers will be able to make financial returns as well as cause impact in the continent in the forms of jobs, as well as improve environmental and social issues and the provision of services that otherwise would not have been possible. In the last ten or so years, impact investing has become a focal point for foundations, non-governmental organizations (NGOs) and high-net-worth individuals (HNWIs).

Traditional investors are also becoming interested at not only looking at the financial return in any transactions, but also looking at the impacts that can be derived from their investments. In the recent past, there has also been a move toward sustainability in businesses where sustainability matters are high on the companies' agenda—all with the hope of making our continent a better place. This has resulted in a number of participants in the sector who are aiming to start businesses that will solve the problems that our world, especially Africa, is facing.

Businesses in the African continent have traditionally not involved themselves in tackling the social challenges that countries face and, for a long period, this was seen as a role of government. Occasionally, a business, in very isolated cases, would involve itself in some sort of philanthropy trying to solve some of these problems. The concern with the philanthropy perspective is that it was considered after the bottom line of the company and was also seen as an extra cost to the business at the expense of the shareholders.

The solving of social problems by business was seen to have direct implications on their economic results. The reason for this is that, traditionally, the role for businesses has been to maximize profits. For example, under neoclassical economics and several management theories, it has been assumed that the role of a business is to maximize economic gains for its shareholders.

Profit maximization relates to the shareholder's theory and is has been in existence for more than two centuries since it was proposed by Adam Smith in his book, *The Wealth of Nations*. In 1970, Milton Friedman argued that the raison d'être for businesses was to ensure that the wealth of its stock-holders is maximized.

In the recent past, the shareholder's theory has been replaced by the stakeholder's theory. The stakeholder's theory advocates other parties being involved in the business ecosystem, including the likes of government, civil society and NGOs, trade unions, communities, financiers, general public, suppliers, employees and customers.

In this case, the shareholders are treated as the ultimate residual benefi-ciary since they are the provider's financial resources for the business. This has resulted in business moving Corporate Social Responsiblity (CSR) from the philanthropy perspective towards a more integrated perspective.

For businesses to be able to address the stakeholder theory, there are a number of variables that businesses need to consider in terms of doing busi-ness and these include: the business caring more about other stakeholders than the shareholders (i.e., assigning importance to stakeholders compared with shareholders); companies looking at their performance more from a long-term perspective as opposed to quarterly and semi-annual perfor-mances; and focusing on the ethical grounds of their decisions.

During the last two decades, more and more companies have voluntarily integrated social and environmental issues in their business strategies as part of the stakeholder's theory integration through corporate sustainability activ-ities. Corporate sustainability (CS) is a way of doing business that embraces opportunities and manages risk from three dimensions: economic, environ-mental and social.

This is CSR in a broader sense than the case of the philanthropy. It implies management is concerned with the activities of the business and how that affects the stakeholders and this not only for the purposes of feel-ing good but also for making money. In other words, CSR is sustainabil-ity that is embedded within the business strategies. The movement towards more than the philanthropy CSR has made the role of business in sustaina-ble development even more relevant.

The introduction of the Sustainable Developement Goals (SDGs) in September 2015 created a platform that will help companies move towards more coordinated CSR, which is more relevant, and which is a win–win for all the parties involved.

Businesses will have no other choice but to move towards more sustaina-ble CSR. This is not only the right thing to do but it is also the right thing to do due to the push by the various interested parties in a business.

As an example, customers and employees are putting immense pres-sure on businesses in demanding integration of the both the social and environmental issues in the business operations. Regulators are also pushing companies to be more ethical from different perspectives.

This approach has now been proven to reward shareholders as there is a correlation between economic performance and corporate social performance and hence shareholders are pushing for the embedment of social and environmental considerations within business strategies.

Start-up ecosystems are emerging in Nairobi, Lagos and Pretoria, all with the aim of producing businesses that will provide goods and services to the people of the African continent.

Although there is a lot of volatility and unpredictability in the market, there is still huge traction to be gained, especially in terms of globalization and digital connectivity. Remember, there are many big dreams that do not see the light of day, and by giving them a chance to become reality we can spread development to areas that really need it—far from the usual development hubs in a country.

Agribusiness is also proving a fertile ground for impact investing, and is particularly a useful tool for spreading development because it takes place far away from the usual development hubs. Simply put, agribusiness can spread development to the rural areas of a country. A good example is a company called Allure Flowers, based in the southern part of Tanzania in a place called Njombe, 500 kilometres from the capital, Dar es Salaam.

Allure Flowers was established by a Danish accountant who had partnered with locals to grow roses. The total investment in the project was US$1 million, which went towards the building of greenhouses and other infrastructure required for a flower-growing farm. The roses are exported to Amsterdam and are usually transported the 500 kilometres to Dar es Salaam overnight to then be shipped to Schiphol.

The value proposition for this case is that due to the high altitude in the Njombe area of Tanzania, the roses have a considerable length advantage over those grown in Arusha, which is the other predominant rose-growing area of Tanzania. These flowers from Njombe are therefore able to attract 100% more in price than the Arusha variety.

The project had the impact of creating over 150 jobs as well as indirectly creating a further 200+ jobs. In addition, the project generates additional revenue for the government of Tanzania through taxes.

In my view, investments such as Allure Flowers are more impactful in ending rural poverty than the top-down straight cash disbursement through programmes that do not follow up to see whether the money is put to the right use, or even gets to the intended recipients.

Large-Scale Impact Investments

It is not just small, scale-up enterprises that can benefit from impact investment. Africa is currently home to some of the biggest infrastructure projects in the world. Good examples are the roads, railways, dams and power projects being developed in almost every corner of Africa.

China has financed—albeit through loans—major railways in Africa with the examples from Kenya and Ethiopia costing to the tune of over US$7 billion each. China has also committed to financing another railway in Ghana for over US$10 billion. The other major investments happening are in the financial sector, hospitality industry (mainly hotels and lodges), and technology-based industries such as the telecommunication sector.

Historically, the level of investment in Africa by foreign parties has been very low. This is mainly due to the perception that the investment risk in Africa is high. In reality, the risks in Africa are not different from those found in other developing markets. This is to say that the level of risk perception for the continent is not the same as the real risk of the continent.

There is definitely a need for investors to carry out due diligence for their potential investments from a risk perspective but, more importantly, they should go into the analysis with an open mind and leave behind the stereotyping that normally indicates that Africa is a continent that represents a risk for investment. In fact, many large and small investments in Africa have defied this myth and have resulted in better returns for those investors who have capitalized on the risk mismatch.

The mis-match between the real risk and the perceived risk presents a business opportunity. In the last 15 years, there has been a mushrooming of funds and investment vehicles that have been set up to harvest the opportunities that are emanating from the challenges facing Africa. In particular, there have been funds focusing on the financial returns in addition to focusing on the social and environmental progress of the continent.

Funding is coming from the public sector in the form of development financial institutions or private sources. The aim of these financing mechanisms is to capture the blended value and the resulting experience has been mixed.

The key point to note is that the challenges facing Africa can be converted to business opportunities. For instance, in 2008, I was working for the Danish International Investment Fund (IFU), a development financial institution that invests on a private sector basis for the Danish State. IFU is part of the European Development Financial Institution (EDFI) and was established in 1967 with the sole aim of investing in developing countries, with objectives relating to both financial returns and development.

One of the flagship projects in East Africa for the IFU at that point was the Lake Turkana Wind Power (LTWP) project, which was aimed at solving the electricity generation gap in Kenya.

Together with other investors, the Danish Fund invested over US$800 million in the 300 megawatts project. The project was to provide over 25% of Kenya's energy needs and this was particularly encouraging as the source of energy was to be green.

This meant that the Kenya's sources of energy were becoming more than 75% green, which is uncommon in Africa and meant better safeguarding of the environment. The other major renewable sources of power for Kenya are hydro energy and geothermal energy.

However, impact investment does not have to occur at this monumental, institutional level. There are meaningful, direct opportunities for impact investment at the other end of the scale. This line of thinking has been the driver behind key plans like the US government's Power for Africa initiative, which aims to put in up to US$7 billion in clean electricity projects that can bridge the huge gap of 600 million Africans who do not have access to energy resources.

The LTWP case is a good example of how impact investing and sustainable development-driven investment can be used to implement changes in the continent.

Sustainable Development Goal 7 (SDG7), Universal Access to Energy, is intricately linked to the attainment of almost all of SDGs, such as employment, education, health, poverty reduction, gender equality, food security, poverty reduction and climate change, to name a few. The Sustainability Development Knowledge Platform estimates that energy access is interconnected to 125 of the 169 (73%) targets of the wider development agenda. This tells us that realizing universal energy access is indispensable to the accomplishment of Agenda 2030.

So what is the challenge and why does it matter for Sub-Saharan Africa? To give a sense of the scope of the energy access hurdles in Sub-Saharan Africa, the World Bank estimates an overwhelming 70% (609 million) of the global population without access to electricity are in Sub-Sahara Africa.[1]

---

[1]World Bank. 2017. *State of Electricity Access Report 2017 (Vol. 2): Full Report (English)*. Washington, DC: World Bank Group.

What is more, the World Bank's 2017 Sustainable Energy Access Report (SEAR 2017)[2] cautions that with the business-as-usual approach, a significant percentage of the population in Sub-Sahara Africa will not receive reliable electricity access by 2030.

The key hurdle in Sub-Saharan Africa remains providing reliable access to electricity that supports productive use; for example, electricity services that support controlled storage to reduce the post-harvest losses experienced by farmers, electricity for rural irrigation and electricity in rural health centres remains limited.

Evidence further points out that power shortages and pricey services cost African economies 2–4% of GDP annually. The overwhelming deficit in electricity access in Sub-Saharan Africa implies that sustainable economic development is challenging—if not impossible—if access to energy is not realized.

The fundamental questions, therefore, remain: how we can accelerate the transition to accessing affordable and reliable electricity? How can the rural farmer access electricity that enhances their income beyond meeting the basic need of lighting? How can we provide reliable electricity to industries in the rural setting but also simultaneously provide reliable electricity to the growing manufacturing sector in the cities? The profound solution lays in enhanced innovativeness in the generation, transmission, and distribution of electricity.

This call for impact investing both in the small scale and in the larger scale coming up with innovative way of channelling the funds to energy companies that will enable the transition to more access to affordable and reliable electricity. All is not gloomy since countries in Sub-Saharan Africa are already setting the wheels in motion to realise SDG 7, Universal Energy Access.

However, the achievements will be realized one step at a time if our economies commit to undertake some of the necessary opportunities that are emerging with electricity supply. Below I will discuss some of the interventions that are profound and that could provide opportunities for the impact investing sector.

Tapping into alternative energy sources would provide one such opportunity. Sub-Saharan Africa has a massive potential of renewable energy

---

[2]World Bank. 2017. *State of Electricity Access Report 2017 (Vol. 2): Full Report (English)*. Washington, DC: World Bank Group.

sources, with solar capacity alone amounting to over 1000 gigawatts. Such a resource would offer insurmountable benefits to the population in addition to mitigating global warming. Expanding the use of renewables such as solar technologies, wind technologies and biofuels therefore becomes imperative and national governments through national strategies and in partnership with the private sector should ensure that these alternative sources of energy are prioritized. Moreover, the declining cost of renewables technology provides an opportunity for the countries and investors to be creative in meeting the persistent electricity challenge.

Sustainable Energy Fund for Africa (SEFA), a multinational donor trust fund that is walking the walk of innovation and is already driving the transition to renewable energy by supporting small- and medium-scale renewable energy in Africa. Such an intervention will reduce the existing high dependence on fossil fuels while aligning future development ambitions with environmental sustainability targets.

Emerging decentralized approaches should also be explored. The increasing rural–urban migration in Sub-Saharan Africa makes the conventional centralized grid system a predominant approach in electrification in urban areas. However, the population in the rural setting will continue to grow, accentuating the significance of decentralized mini-grid solutions in ensuring universal electricity access.

The plummeting cost of solar and hydro mini-grids due to technology improvements and the increasing penetration of Pay As You Go (PAYG) systems makes mini-grids more attractive for remote households that are sparsely distributed.

However, complementarity of the conventional centralized and the emerging decentralized system is a key issue that would need to be addressed for the long-term sustainability of the decentralized systems.

It is important to create an enabling regulatory environment. Emerging models in the delivery of electricity entail an increased role of the private sector and impact investing in terms of providing the form of financing and service integration that demands incentives that de-risks and guarantees return on investments.

Policies on electricity wheeling, feed-in tariffs, and renewable electricity auctions have to be well instituted in order to support the emerging models and value chains and attract more investment in electricity supply value chain.

SEFA, discussed above, is one of the initiatives that is driving this movement in Africa. Drawing from the regulatory approach of mobile money in East Africa, the electricity regulators would adopt a test-and-learn approach to catalyse the commercial roll-out of emerging unproven business models in the electricity market.

Investing in skills revolution will play an important role. An underlying challenge in universal electricity access is deeply rooted in the deficit of expatriates within Sub-Saharan Africa. The pool of skilled people who can embrace the emerging energy technologies remains minimal, which is mainly attributable to the excessive brain drain. On the other hand, adaptation to local dynamics will play a central role in universal electricity access and this will be guaranteed by a pool of local expertise.

Therefore, it is paramount to institute initiatives aimed at reversing the outflow of African expertise and retention and retraining the current pool of expertise within the continent. The Open Africa Power Initiative by Enel Foundation in partnership with Strathmore University is one platform that is promoting targeted skills development by retraining expatriates in the energy sector.

In conclusion, with regard to this example of energy access, we ought to appreciate that universal access to reliable and affordable electricity is a challenge that touches everyone and confronts every country.

The bottom line is that innovative approaches in technologies and business models and partnerships provide the pathway that will close the gap when it comes to accessing affordable, reliable and sustainable electricity services in sub-Saharan Africa, removing a key hurdle in the realization of Agenda 2030.

Even with innovation, we have to carefully manage the potential trade-off between the speed and sustainability of electrification acceleration efforts so as to simultaneously guarantee quality and quantity.

The role of developed countries should not always be about the hard cash investments that are being made in the continent; there is need for the West and other developed countries who have large, developed markets, to provide a share of their domestic markets to African companies. This can be achieved by making accommodative policies that allow for African goods to enter their market, and in the process help to create thousands of jobs on the continent. A good example of this is the AGOA pact between the USA and Africa, which has helped support the textile industry in a few countries.

By enhancing the enabling environments for the manufactures, the continent will become a manufacturing hub, which will result in the attraction of more investment funds into the continent to provide the required financing for the manufacturing sector place due to the need for financing from companies being provided with the enabling environment. On the other hand, once manufacturing is booming, there will be more and more jobs created and increased disposable income, among other impact returns.

Ending Poverty Through Impact Investments

Considering the level of poverty in the continent, there are definitely many areas where impact investing can be of help. These are areas where governments have failed to provide solutions and the private sector can come up with innovations and business systems that may be able to develop some social good and, at the same time, make some reasonable returns.

In the recent past, there has been a lot of interest in impact investing in Africa as this is seen as way to address the challenges that face the continent. Impact investing has a significant potential to contribute to African economic growth and development. Financial flows have been on the rise in the last decade in Africa.

Unfortunately, the financial flows have not been sufficiently used in the provisions that address the challenges faced by the continent. There is a need to have the flows tapped to provide goods and services that address the African development challenges.

Governments must also ensure that there is an enabling environment that will attract financing for development in order to enable the continent to be able to get to the 2030 Agenda and at the same time achieve the African vision 2063.

It is evident that impact investing provides the opportunity for the African continent to develop. This will be through the complementation of public spending and development assistance by bringing in private sector funding and skills to reduce the vulnerability of African economies to external shocks. It is also about providing broad-based solutions to address environmental and social needs.

It will provide the opportunity for the public as well as ODA financing to focus on those social and environmental needs that cannot be implemented in a market-based approach. My estimation is that we are still in the early days and more is expected on the impact investing space.

More financial flows and innovations are expected as more impact investors and impact-related entrepreneurs thrive in the continent. Financing in the sector will come from a variety of sources, which will include the traditional private equity and asset management funds, development financial institutions (DFIs), foundations and family offices, as well as other institutional investors.

For the impact investing sector to become robust in Africa, it will be necessary to create an enabling environment that will help in the development of the impact investing sector. Impact investing is faced with myriad of challenges within the African context raging from access to the deals, lack of an ecosystem that will help the deals to thrive, as well as lack of a proper exit mechanism, among other challenges that will be highlighted later in this book.

The discussion point for African governments will be how to make impact investing more attractive in order to mobilize more capital as well as the skills needed to assist in resolving the poverty levels in Africa. Governments needs to have working sessions that will make impact investing vibrant in their respective countries.

Some countries are clearly taking the lead, with Kenya, Tanzania, South Africa and Ghana making the greatest progress down this route. At the same time, there is need for the entrepreneurs and innovators to come up with ideas that will be bankable and hence provide a strong pipeline of deals that will be able to satisfy the financial, social and environmental requirements of the providers of capital.

When these two parameters are in place, the role of the government will be to enable the ecosystem so that the two sides—the financiers and the entrepreneurs—can be matched. This calls for an enabling environment created through the right rules and regulations as well as some incentives that will help the sector to thrive. As such, there is a case for using investment as a means of ending poverty in Africa.

It is good to note that there have been big improvements across Africa over the last 50 years, from a development perspective. Most of the development indicators have increased, especially in the last 15 years. Some of the key indicators that have seen significant improvements include; literacy levels, health sector, infrastructure, growth of GDP, and food security, among others.

Despite the considerable positive change in the indicators noted above, the levels of poverty are still high and much more needs to be done. The hoped effect of development is the improvement of the poverty index through an increase in disposable income and also improvement in the distribution of wealth. One of the fundamental challenges to development in Africa has been the distribution of wealth amongst the populace. The 80–20 or should I say the 90–10 rule seems to be very alive in Africa and there are those that have argued that this could even be lower. This rule indicates that 90% of the wealth is owned by 10% of the population. I believe that this could be even lower and that, in fact, an even smaller percentage of the African population holds 90% of the wealth.

The development progress in Africa seen in the last decade has been achieved due to the mix of interventions from various players such as the government, development partners, multilateral organizations such as the

World Bank and IMF, private sector, civil society and academia who have worked relentlessly to make the African continent a better place. However, it is important to note that the interventions by the aforementioned players have not always resulted in positive movement toward development.

Much needs to be done in Africa, especially considering what other developing continents have achieved during the same period. Africa's development has not been commensurate with other developing regions due to a number of factors.

These range from lack of proper development planning from the countries' perspectives, lack of the relevant interventions, overreliance on aid and development partners-driven interventions as opposed to Africa- and private sector-owned strategies, lack of the existing private sector in the engagement on the development agenda and the volatile politics in most of the African continent. Due to the above, there is a definite need for innovative intervention if we are going to end poverty in Africa in the next 15 years as promised by the SDGs or the Agenda 2030.

Some of the interventions required will include improvements in the education systems, improvement in health services delivery, providing food security mechanisms, provision of energy and energy services, improvement of gender equality, provision of clean drinking water, addressing the effect of climate change as well as mitigating the same, and provision of infrastructure, among others.

Development aid has been the main way that development partners have been helping to address the gaps identified in terms of the continent moving towards development. In some instances, this has worked and in others it has been a disaster. There is need to learn from the past mistakes that the donor communities have experienced but, more importantly, there is need to have some innovation in the way the development assistance is provided, especially with the aim of the sustainability of the programs and involvement of the locals.

The private sector needs to be involved in the development agenda in Africa and embracing the Sustainable Development Goals by the African private sector will play a key role. By companies embedding SDGs in their strategies, it is possible that most of the development parameter will be achieved in the next 15 years, hence helping Africa to achieve the Agenda 2030.

The intervention by the private sector should involve both the Multinational Corporations (MNCs), big African corporates, Small and Medium Enterprises (SMEs) as well as the informal sector. The informal sector accounts for over 70% of jobs in Africa and hence presents a huge potential in creating even more jobs if interventions that will strengthen the sector are put in place.

The interventions may include innovative financing of the informal sector, capacity building and training, provision of facilities that will be relevant to improving efficiency as well as the government providing an enabling environment for these interventions to operate.

The informal sector vibrancy in most of Africa is due to the entrepreneurial spirit in the continent. This is at its highest level in the twenty-first century and is characterized by the fact that most of the people including those in full time employment have a side hustle that generates some cash only that full attention is not provided by the 'entrepreneur' in question.

This means that the African continent is faced with an opportunity to get relevant solutions to its challenges through the encouragement of the entrepreneurial spirit in the continent, which could be done through the social entrepreneurship and impacting investing supporting mechanisms including investing.

There are proven cases that have demonstrated that this is indeed possible. Later in the book, I will be sharing some of these cases on how innovation, including technological, business models and financing innovations have a made a difference for a continent that has been lagging behind for the last 50 years.

These interventions when made sustainable can resolve many challenges that the continent is faced with, especially if done from a sustainability perspective. This means that businesses, impact investors, high-net-worth individuals and foundations, as well as development partners, should consider engaging in social entrepreneurship and innovations for the purpose of resolving social challenges but more importantly to make some reasonable returns.

The definition for return here goes beyond financial returns since not all parties listed above are keen to achieve a financial returns but rather could be interested in other forms of returns. The other forms of returns that may be relevant include social returns, environmental-related returns or prosperity returns. Another area that can bear fruits in helping African development to rise to the next level is addressing the governance challenge. Good governance is a key condition for development in any developing country and this especially true in Africa.

There is need to have a mechanism of governance where most, if not all stakeholders are involved in the national development for the purpose of transparency and accountability in the allocation and use of public funds as well as policy management. Governance should also focus on the ways that the leaders are elected in countries to ensure that the right leaders are elected and hence will be able to manage the affairs of the countries in the best way possible.

The intervention in governance will also need to be innovative as various traditional methods have previously been used and they did not result in much progress, other than agitation, from the African leaders who felt that the interventions were imposed upon them. This is the way forward for Africa's development partners if the continent is to be lifted from its chronic dependence on handouts.

Looking back, in the twentieth century, some of the best interventions by the developed nations in Africa involved cases where real investments as opposed to grants took the centre stage. A case in point is the work carried out by the development financial institutions in Africa with investments in agribusiness, infrastructure and manufacturing and services industries resulting in millions of jobs and at the same time generating billions of US dollars paid in as taxes to governments for the provisions of the public goods.

This means that private investment has the possibility to create the desired development in Africa. Investment should not be viewed as colonization part two, where the Western world will transfer all proceeds or profits to their capitals. This, unfortunately, has been the case for some time with the advent of transfer pricing and other profit-concealing mechanisms. Care must be taken to eradicate these bad habits.

Private sector investments should chase returns since they are readily available in Africa but more importantly there is need to share the value with all the stakeholders involved in such investments, including the government as well as the host communities.

There is also need for some innovation among the development agencies and foundations that are restricted from private investments. In these cases, other softer ways of investing should be considered, such as engaging with mission-driven organisations that are not there primarily for returns but rather for social good and empowering citizens. This will result in the sustainability of the initiatives that are implemented on the ground, thereby increasing the longevity of the interventions as well as the expected impact. The new trajectory will also result in the multipliers effects, since the interventions will have long-standing benefits for the economies in Africa.

As investments in the form of Foreign Direct Investment (FDI) are directed to Africa, there is need to emphasize the point that agriculture and commodities are not the only ways to invest in Africa.

As noted elsewhere in this book, health care, education, IT technologies, manufacturing, housing and financial services are other sectors that make a compelling case for investment and at the same time for solving the challenges of the continent. In reality, the investment risks in Africa are no different from those in other developing markets. In reality, the actual risk in Africa is much less that the perceived risks. In fact, many large and small investments in Africa have defied this myth, resulting in to better returns for those investors who have capitalized on the risk mismatch.

The possibility of many options in terms of sectors for investments presents a business opportunity. In the last 15 years, there has been mushrooming of funds and investment vehicles that have been set up to harvest the opportunities that are emanating from the challenges facing Africa. In particular, there have been funds that are focusing on the financial returns as well as on the social and environmental progress of the continent. The funding is coming from the public sector in the form of development financial institutions or private sources. The aim of these financing mechanisms is to capture the blended value and the resulting experience has been mixed.

The key point to note is that the challenges facing Africa can be converted to business opportunities.

What Is the Best Possible Solution for Africa?

Private sector and market-driven interventions will definitely play a key role in the economic development of the African continent.

The traditional private sector intervention has played a significant role in the development in Africa, especially where the business model is straight forward.

However, the matter is complicated when it relates to the provision of social or public good. In most instances, the citizens and the private sector have expected this to be provided by the government of the day.

Unfortunately, this has not been the case due to the limited resources. To bridge the gap, the emergence of social and mission-driven enterprises have been on the rise and these have a huge potential in moving developing countries towards development and, at the same time, in solving those challenges being faced by such developing countries.

There has been a huge global movement toward impact investing, which is giving rise to social enterprises aimed at solving the challenges on a market-based that will have otherwise been resolved by government.

Impact investing in Africa remains nascent and has the potential to resolve the African challenges, especially in health, education social services, provision of energy and so on, and at the same time contribute to the continent's objectives surrounding economic growth and development. As noted above, in the past, the African continent was focused on official development assistance (ODA) from developed and other emerging markets, in order to meet the basic service needs of their populations.

Due to the shocks and challenges facing the global economies, it is expected that ODA will no longer be the major source of development financing in developing countries. Private sources of capital will play a larger role, where it will be used to improve access to social services in Africa.

In the last decade, there has been a significant increase in the private financial flows to Africa as the traditional ODA declines. This will mean that there is need for the African governments to provide the relevant space to attract even more private funding, especially where those funds will be able to provide for public goods in a market-based approach.

This will be of help in addressing the socio-economic challenges by providing market-based solutions that address the priority areas such as health, education, water and energy supplies, among others. Impact investment has the potential to fill in the above space and to complement public spending and ODA.

This will be achieved by bringing in private sector capital and skills to reduce African economies' vulnerability to external shocks, providing a market-based solution to address socio-economic needs, and allowing ODA in flows and public spending to focus on addressing social needs for which there is currently no viable market-based solution. Sometimes the impact investor, be it a company, ODA or philanthropic unit, needs an experienced hand on the ground to help them reach the entrepreneur who is in need of their funds.

One of the poorer areas on the continent is the Great Lakes Region. This area is home to some of the longest running conflicts in Africa, all the while sitting on some of the most fantastic natural resource ecosystems in the world.

Msingi East Africa Limited, an impact investing firm that is actively involved in supporting firms that are deemed transformative in their field in the East Africa region, is working hard to point the millions living here in the right direction, at least as far as enterprise is concerned. The company has narrowed down to various sectors, and aquaculture is one of them. Aquaculture, an arm of agriculture focuses on water-based farming. In East Africa, they focus on fish, mainly tilapia and catfish, even though they support other farmers who are doing trout and sea weed farming.

Msingi is supporting entrepreneurs' access or build a stock of good quality genetics for fish, basically building a pedigree just like in dairy farming. They ultimately want to build a resilient market (access to market) for what is expected to be a high-growth investment. To raise the quality of fish, they help the farmers improve the quality of fish feed and make sure that hatcheries are able to provide quality fingerlings to a wide area.

Msingi is active in Kenya, Uganda, Tanzania and Rwanda, with its stated outcomes also including a drive for increased consumption of fish by citizens, and therefore also impacting on the nutrition of the population by increasing protein sources. On a higher impact level, they are looking to build more jobs as farms grow and new players come into the industry. As the supply chain grows, they will also create additional jobs.

This firm is a good example of scaling down ODA funds to provide local solutions, reaching more people than an official sitting, say, in London would, while carrying out direct investments in Africa. In order to fight poverty, investors therefore need to establish partnerships with local firms that have localized knowledge, not just of the markets, but also of the local problems at the forefront of any impact investor's mind.

By using this approach, the investor also gains from accessing a ready market since business is all about identifying a gap, providing a solution for it and making money in the process.

Msingi has existed as a company since 2017, and as a programme for the three years prior to this. It is funded by the British government through the Department for International Development (DfID), and the British foundation Gatsby Africa, which was founded in 1967 by Lord David Sainsbury, a British businessman, politician and philanthropist. The company thus provides a useful link between the financing institution, and the final recipient of the funds—the small-scale fish farmer—who would probably have never been able to state their case to the DfID or Gatsby Africa.

In Conclusion

Often, the biggest hurdle for an impact business to overcome is delivering the change they desire to the community. For an enterprise, making a profit is perhaps the easier thing to achieve, given that this is what businesses are made for in the first place!

In this chapter of this book, we have explored the different ways that a business can ensure that there is trickle down of its gains to the community in which it operates—essentially the very definition of impact investment.

I will now list some of the important takeaways that I feel should be at the back of the mind of every investor when they are setting up their business.

The ideas that an investor comes up with should be bankable, which will mean that they will provide a strong pipeline of deals that will be able to satisfy both the providers of capital, and the recipients of the impact that is sought in the community.

In doing this, investors should learn from the past mistakes that the donor communities have experienced in Africa, and at the same time should observe how they are carrying out development assistance, since the methods have been refined based on past failure.

The private sector needs to be involved in the development agenda in Africa and embracing the Sustainable Development Goals by the African private sector will play a key role. Therefore, we have said that impact investors should incorporate SDGs in their strategies.

Another issue that will be a recurring theme in this book is the governance problem that affects most young start-ups in Africa. These family-owned businesses often have a problem transiting from a one-man show to a corporate structure where decisions are made in a more collegiate way.

Good corporate governance is a key condition for development in any developing country and this is especially the case in Africa.

Addressing these issues will ensure that the goals of impacting society will be achieved. As we shall see in chapter seven, it is easier to measure and quantify impact when there are clear lines of structure in a business.

Remember it is also important to share value with all the stakeholders involved in such investment, including the incumbent government as well as the host communities. This is often the easiest way to ensure that there is tangible impact. However, in conclusion, ensuring impact is not exclusively the domain of the investor.

Governments and policy makers must also provide an enabling environment that will attract financing for development in order to enable the countries achieve their development goals. Through this, they are able to complement public spending and development assistance with private sector funding and skills, all for the good of their populace. I also see impact investing as an opportunity to focus on those social and environmental needs that cannot be implemented in a market-based approach.

Keeping this in mind, let us now look at the landscape of impact investing in Africa, to see where the continent is at this moment in time after more than a decade of being one of the major recipients of this type of funding.

4

Landscape of Impacting Investing in Africa

There is a significant demand for investment solutions that will help with deploying capital in a more sustainable and impact-driven way for development purposes. The African continent has not been left behind in this movement and the impact investing sector is growing at a tremendous rate.

The rates of growth are even higher than those of traditional investments. This growth is signified by both the funds under management as well as the number of impact funds operating in the continent. The funds are attracted to different impacts as per their investment thesis. Environmental impact-related funds have the highest market share, with more than 55% of the funds operating in the continent targeting environmental returns.

Funds looking for combined social and environmental returns account for about 35% of the market share with the difference of 10% being those funds that are only attracted to social returns.

My prediction is that, in the coming years, we will see more and more funds targeting social issues such as health, education, security and conflict.

In 2017, there were close to 230 impact investment vehicles operating in Africa. Some fund managers are managing more than one investment vehicle and hence the number of fund managers involved is a little lower than the number of funds.

The Global Impact Investing Network (GIIN) reports that in 2017, sub-Saharan Africa accounted for 10% of the total of US$113 billion deployed in impact investments globally.[1] This share is growing quickly.

---

[1]Global Impact Investing Network (GIIN).

© The Author(s) 2018
E. Mungai, *Impact Investing in Africa*,
https://doi.org/10.1007/978-3-030-00428-6_4

Out of 209 respondents to a survey carried out by GIIN in 2017, 95 said they would be looking to deploy funds in Africa, second only to the 97 who said they were intending to deploy funds in the USA and Canada.

Impact managers will take the form of development financial institutions (DFIs), impact fund managers, family offices, foundations, commercial banks and other diversified financial institutions and angel networks. The hot spots for impact investing in Africa are Kenya, Nigeria, Ghana, Rwanda and South Africa—economies that are either the largest on the continent (South Africa and Nigeria) or the most dynamic (Kenya, Rwanda and Ghana). These economies have been receiving the bulk of the funds under management as well as acting as the impact investors' chosen locations.

As with other areas of the world, DFIs have accounted for the lion's share of the funds under management as well as the number of the deals that received investment in 2017. DFIs invest both as direct investments or as funds of funds which means putting funds into smaller funds that have a specific expertise in a given area.

An example of this is Kinyeti Venture Capital. This is an investment company that is mission driven; it makes equity and loan investments in profitable enterprises in South Sudan.

Enterprises should provide not just a financial return but, more importantly, they should be able to deliver impacts in the form of jobs and better livelihoods for the people of South Sudan as well as environmental benefits.

Kinyeti Venture Capital was established in 2012 as a joint venture between two DFIs, Norfund and SwedFund. To date, most of the investments have been in the form of debt or debt-like investment as opposed to equity and equity-like investment. This signifies that the investors are still risk averse in the exposures on the Africa continent, mainly due to the passive risk as opposed to the real risk. Investment exit challenges are real due to the limited number of exit possibilities, which in turn has affected the instruments that the investors can use in order to deploy their financing. More of these issues will be covered under the challenges of impact investing in Africa in Chapter 8 of this book.

In the recent past, there has been a movement to have private investors such as pension funds synergizing with the DFIs in order to make investments in the developing countries, with aim of providing pensioners and other investors in Europe and USA with returns that have a purpose.

In 2011 while at the Danish International Investment Funds (IFU), we innovated a model aimed at attracting the Danish pension funds for impact investments. This resulted in the need for collaboration between traditional investors and those who had some experiences in managing impact businesses.

The first such collaboration involved the Danish Microfinance Partners and a US$90 million fund for the purposes of investing in micro-financing institutions in Africa, Asia and Latin America. The fund was co-managed by both IFU (Investeringsfonden for Udviklingslande—Investment Fund for Developing Countries) and Maj Invest, a traditional investment management company, on behalf of the Danish state and the pensioners.

In the recent past, nontraditional impact investors are moving into the impact investing space through the creation of funds that are dedicated to specific sectors for impact. These include climate funds and agricultural funds within the Danish DFI. Importantly, other DFIs are engaging with education funds, climate funds, health funds and housing, among other areas.

For those looking at impact investing in Africa, the choice of route for investment (through DFI or through a non-DFI investor) will depend on a number of considerations. Such considerations will include the size of the investment, the sector and the experience required to invest in the targeted sector, financial return requirements, impact required and the level of sophistication of the investor, investment instrument required, possibilities of exits, the risk appetite and the stage of development of the companies that the investor is looking to invest in.

The business growth stage, as mentioned above, is a key element that determines if the investee company will receive financing from the impact investors. The development stage will include the start-up stage where the business will require seed capital; at the post-revenue stage but before the growth stage, the business will require venture capital; at the growth stage, the company will require growth capital; and after the maturity stage, there will be different sources as well as instruments that the investors can use to invest in the businesses.

Seed stage investment has not been as popular with the impact investors as they mostly invest in the growth stage and the post-revenue stage. This is an indicator that they still do not have the risk appetite that is exhibited by venture capital and private equity funds, which have a more aggressive investment style. When it comes to financial returns, impact investing must be sustainable in providing some market return to the investors. Indeed, most of the impact investors are looking for an above- or near-market return.

Very few cases are looking for capital preservation. On average, impact funds have provided investors with percentage returns that are in the double digits. At the same time, the impact resulting from the investment is even greater since investee companies create jobs and provide social services or protect the environment.

As one invests in Africa, it will not be unreasonable to request 10% financial returns in addition to a demonstrated social or environmental impact by the investment.

Impact businesses are providing impact to the masses by ensuring that we are providing to the bottom of the pyramid (BoP) market segment. This has become one of the key attractions for impact investing and investors are always on the lookout for those businesses that are addressing the needs of the BoP. This has resulted in many impact investors working in the informal sectors as well as other locations, which concentrate on the BoP constituents.

The business sectors that are attractive ranges from retail, housing, health, education, water and other social services. There is also an expected rise in climate-related sectors such as renewable and climate-smart agriculture, which will provide citizens with increased access to power and more sustainable agriculture.

Who Is Investing in the African Impact Investing Space?

There are different investors in the space who have different investment motivations. DFIs are the most active in this space, and others include foundations, family offices, insurance companies, banks, diversified financial institutions, pension funds, and high-net-worth persons.

Foundations

Foundations will include both family and corporate foundations. The space is mainly dominated by European and North American foundations. Some of the household names that are investing in Africa include Calvert, Citi, DOEN, Ford, Lundin, Omidyar, Gates, Gatsby, MacArthur and Rockefeller foundations. Different foundations will have different rationales for investing, taking into account aspects such as returns, sectors, expected impact and philanthropic motivation.

For instance, the foundations from Europe are more open to donations, whilst those from the USA will be looking for market or near-market returns for their investments.

Most of the foundations have joined GIIN. Foundations, especially the ones from USA, also have concessionary programmes, such as the Bill and

Melinda Gates Foundation investments in health and women enterprise. The Ford and Rockefeller foundations also invest in programmes that bring about social change through governance.

In many instances, foundations have played the role of supporting the ecosystems for impact investing as well as capacity building in order to unlock the potential of impact investing in Africa.

A good example is the Shell Foundation's investment in African Small and Medium Enterprises (SMEs) through GroFin, a fund that aspires to support start-ups in expanding their operations, assets and new products in instances where they do not have the collateral that would allow them access to ordinary credit lines or bank loans. GroFin is active in Uganda, Kenya, Nigeria, Ghana, Egypt, Zambia, South Africa, Tanzania and Rwanda, where it normally offers loans valued at between US$100,000 and US$1.5 million to businesses that have a turnover of up to US$15 million, and assets of up to US$6 million.

Foundations are also collaborating with other private investors and DFIs, as they look to raise their operational capacity in deal origination, conducting due diligence and investing. Through such collaborations, foundations are also able to attract and de-risk investment capital from commercial investors and, in some instances, bring in homegrown foundations to the fold.

Some key foundations in Africa that have come into the space in recent years include the Tony Elumelu Foundation in Nigeria, which invests in entrepreneurship programs across Africa and is one of the biggest enablers of youth entrepreneurship on the continent. The Aga Khan Foundation, with deep roots in East Africa, works with its sister economic development organization to invest in microfinance and other financial products for the poor and for independent media and local energy production facilities in Africa and Asia, creating thousands of jobs as well as having other impacts.

Pension Funds and Insurers

Pension funds traditionally provide long-term and patient capital. Recently, pension funds have emerged as a major driver in the impact investing space, especially over the last 10 years. Some governments have also actively supported the mobilization of pension funds for impact investing.

In the UK, Investing4Growth Fund (I4G) has shown the way for such endeavors. This fund is made up of five local government pension funds, which have committed GB£250 million collectively to go towards socially and environmentally impactful investments. Although I4G mainly invests in the UK, there is no reason that other funds cannot replicate this model and invest in Africa.

Collective investments also offer more scope in expertise, and sharing the risk of such investments mitigates the fears of contributors over new markets. However, the pension funds investing in Africa are doing so working with fund managers and private equity funds, which mostly have a boots-on-the-ground approach in Africa through their regional offices. This is because most impact investing opportunities in developing countries have been smaller in size and shorter term in nature, providing mixed rates of return, and sometimes unclear prospects for exit. By contrast, pension funds require large-scale, lower risk, long-term investments that yield market-rate returns and have clear exit pathways.

The insurance industry has also shown an increased propensity for green and climate investment driven by the opportunity to offset investments against savings from fewer insurance claims and lower insurance. More insurance companies are also adopting the UN Principles of Responsible Insurers, which calls for the insurers to support sustainable and inclusive economic and social development.

Banks

Although banks have traditionally been motivated by profits and not by the impact of the investments they lend to, they are increasingly finding it hard to ignore the social and environmental aspects of the investments they support. It is for this reason that some 80 banks in 35 countries (27 in developing or emerging countries) have adopted the Equator Principles (EP), a risk-management framework that helps bank determine, assess and manage the environmental and social risk of the projects they finance.

The EP Association was formed in 2010, and it seeks to provide a minimum standard for due diligence carried out on projects by affiliates to determine that the projects they are financing meet the required environmental and social impact thresholds. A growing number of banks are also financing environmentally sustainable projects by participating in lending through green bonds.

Initiative Climate Bonds says that the green bonds market, which was established in 2007, has really taken off in the last five years, with issuances rising from US$11 billion in 2013 to US$157 billion in 2017. One of the requirements of a green bond is that the issuer must monitor and report on how the proceeds are being put to use in a sustainable manner, unlike ordinary bonds where the only obligation of the issuer is to repay the money at the stipulated time.

Banks in developed countries are also using their wealth management arms to partner in impact investment projects and offer solutions to their clients in this field of investment.

Lenders such as JP Morgan, UBS, German private bank Berenberg, Deutsche Bank and Citibank have been offering microfinance and impact investment products for more than a decade.

DFIs such as International Finance Corporation (IFC); Kreditanstalt für Wiederaufbau formerly KfW Bankengruppe (KfW), and the African Developement Bank (AfDB) are also providing credit lines and technical assistance to local commercial banks in order to increase debt finance for Micro, Small & Medium Enterprises (MSME), renewable energy and efficiency finance, women entrepreneurs or finance to entrepreneurs in disadvantaged regions. For instance, in Africa, IFC has been among the most active lenders to banks that have dedicated credit lines for women, youth and enterprise finance.

Sovereign Wealth Funds

Sovereign wealth funds are acknowledged as a major source of foreign direct investment. Their large impact on capital movement has seen them emerge as an important source of flows for impact investments, either investing directly or through fund managers or private equity.

The best known and largest sovereign fund in the world, the Norwegian Government Pension Fund Global (GPFG), which has over US$1 trillion in assets and investments in over 8000 companies, has struck a strong note for sustainable investments by shunning companies whose products cause environmental damage, who are engaged in corrupt practices, and who violate human rights.

This trajectory has increasingly been borrowed by other sovereign funds, with the net effect being that they are better able to identify investees who meet the proper standards.

Multinationals

Multinational firms operating in Africa are also playing a part in impact investments, and not just through their social service programmes, which, for a long time have been nothing more than glorified marketing and publicity platforms.

They are now setting up serious funds that are pumping billions into impactful projects along their value chain whether in agribusiness, energy, healthcare or financial services.

Schneider Electric Energy Access Fund was established in 2009 by Schneider Electric headquartered in Rueil-Malmaison in France. Since then, it has deployed more than €6 million in projects that have helped thousands in Africa access clean energy. French dairy firm Danone in 2009 established a €100 million Ecosystem Fund to finance smallholder actors in its value chain. The fund has led to the creation of more than 70 projects in 30 countries across Africa.

The Pearson Affordable Learning fund helps educate more than 125,000 children in South Africa, Ghana, Kenya, Tanzania, Nigeria, India and the Philippines. Other such funds that have been set up in recent years to drive this line of investment include the Adidas greenENERGY fund and Hydra Ventures fund.

In 2014, British multinational Unilever successfully raised a £250 million green bond to fulfil its core strategic aim of halving its environmental footprint (while doubling turnover) by 2020—money that is also finding its way into the firm's African operations.

These funds have explored opportunities for value creation through partnerships with social and green ventures as a source of innovation and access to new market segments or have started using a corporate venture-investing approach for impact investing.

Diaspora

For Africa, the Diaspora communities in Western and Asian countries are an important source of financing, not just for consumption but also for investments in the African continent. In order to tap this important source of funds, which in 2017 was estimated at US$38 billion by the World Bank, impact investors have developed specific retail products targeting the diaspora, such as the Diaspora Community Initiative by Calvert Impact Capital.

This initiative seeks out impact investment opportunities for Africans in the diaspora community to invest in Africa, supporting small businesses in sectors such as agribusiness, healthcare and education. Organizations such as United States Agency for International Development (USAID) and Overseas Private Investment Corporation (OPIC) are also actively reaching out to the US-based diaspora communities to guide some of their considerable capital capacity towards projects in Africa.

Retail Investors

Ordinary citizens are a category of impact investors that is often over-looked. There are many individuals who are involved in impact investing or who are looking for ways to be involved, and they need to be co-opted even as investees consider bigger funds from abroad. Lending and equity crowdfunding platforms such as global microfinance platform Kiva, which has approximately US$6 billion in capital origination, are providing this opportunity.

Intellecap Impact Investing Network I3N of India is also successfully engaging both experienced investors and inexperienced individuals in the impact investing field.

Closing Thoughts

Sub-Saharan Africa, as we have seen, is now one of the hottest spots for impact investing in the world.

GIIN statistics have shown us that the region now accounts for 10% cent of the total of US$113 billion deployed in impact investments globally, a significant number considering the challenges that people face when setting up businesses on the continent.

In summary, the hot spots for impact investing are Kenya, Nigeria, Ghana, Rwanda and South Africa, with these economies offering either size (Nigeria and South Africa) or dynamism and an educated labor force (Kenya, Ghana and Rwanda). We have also looked at the most popular forms of financing for impact investments, this being debt or debt-like investment as opposed to equity and equity-like investment.

The takeaway from all this is that while Africa retains a front-row position in terms of opportunity for impact investors, those putting in capital remain wary of the potential pitfalls and are looking to minimize risk. However, I contend that, in Africa, it is passive risk rather than real risk that investors will encounter. Investment exit challenges are real due to the limited number of exit possibilities, which in turn has affected the instruments that the investors can use in order to deploy their financing.

We have also mentioned that the continent is still offering some of the highest returns on investment available anywhere around the globe, and therefore an impact investor asking for, say, 10% in financial returns would not be unreasonable.

Finally, it is important to ask: who are the key players in the African impact investment space? Knowing who is investing is important because by studying their investment track record, their preferences and their guidelines, it is possible to get a feel for the impact investing space in Africa even before leaving the office in London or Berlin to go into Africa to explore the opportunities.

We have seen that there are different investors in the space who have different investment motivations. DFIs, given their base mandate of marrying development with investment, are the most active in this space.

In recent years, we have seen family foundations carving out their niche in the investment space, perhaps emboldened by the fact that these investments can meet their goals of both philanthropy and sustainable returns.

Some of the household names that are investing in Africa include Calvert, Citi, DOEN, Ford, Lundin, Omidyar, Gates, Gatsby, MacArthur and Rockefeller foundations, which are putting in billions of dollars into key sectors such as education, healthcare, youth and women empowerment, water and environment conservation.

Other important players in the impact investment space include family offices, insurance companies, banks, diversified financial institutions, pension funds, and high-net-worth persons. Africans living in the diaspora community are also making a strong contribution, and are increasingly aware that they can earn returns while helping their people back home.

It is said that in order to know where you are going, you must know where you are coming from. Now that we have charted how far we have come in the landscape of impact investments in Africa—the key players and the demographics—we can cast our eyes forward and examine the trends we expect to see in the next decade or two in this noble space.

In making the projections of these trends, I have drawn from the experiences I have had in the field over the last few years.

5

Emerging Trends in Impact Investing in Africa

Now that Africa has emerged as the hotbed of impact investing in the world, players in the sector on the African continent are breaking new ground and setting trends that will define impact investment over the next decade.

Having looked at the landscape of impact investing in Africa in the previous chapter, we shall now consider the merging trends for this noble investment option on the African continent, relying heavily on case studies to show how the future of impact investing is shaping up in Africa.

According to the GIIN annual report for 2017, close to 210 investors had invested a total of US$114 billion in various geographies and sectors. Sub-Saharan Africa accounted for over 10% of this portfolio, which was the third largest allocation after USA and Europe.

More and more investors are interested in investing in the African continent as they foresee better impact results as well as better financial returns. This increased level of interest is indicated by many of the fund managers establishing a presence in various parts of the African continent, predominantly in East Africa and West Africa. Nairobi remains the central hub for impact investing in Sub-Saharan Africa and many of the investors have their regional offices based in Nairobi. This is mainly due to the connectivity of Africa from Nairobi as well as the fact that many advisers and ecosystem players are located in Nairobi with the aim of serving the rest of the continent.

The growth in impact investing in the continent is expected to be around 20% year-on-year and I expect this growth to continue over the next 15 years.

© The Author(s) 2018
E. Mungai, *Impact Investing in Africa*,
https://doi.org/10.1007/978-3-030-00428-6_5

This growth is driven by a better enabling environment but more importantly by the move towards more sustainable development-based financing in the continent.

We shall lay down ten of the most visible emerging trends in impact investing, which will give an indication of where the industry is headed and where it will be in the next decade.

Cross-Border Investments Are Becoming More Popular

Most the African countries in isolation do not present a market for products and services that have a significant scale. For businesses to achieve scale, they will have to look outside their borders; this is mainly due to limited population sizes.

Nigeria, with a population of about 185 million people, represents the biggest market. Nigeria, Ethiopia, Democratic Republic of the Congo, South Africa and Egypt are the top five most populous countries in the African continent, accounting for more than 40% of the African population.

Social businesses and impact investors are therefore looking for deals that will be cross border as this will increase the level of impact as well as the financial returns of the business, mainly due to the economies of scale.

A good example is the SimGas Limited, which was established in 2009. SimGas initially started in Tanzania and now is looking at expanding into Kenya. SimGas is a commercial biogas company that develops, sells and installs biogas digesters for dairy farmers in East Africa with the aim of making a financial return and at the same time using the concept of biogas to save lives due to reduced indoor pollutants—saving time for African women as well as mitigating climate change.

To date, SimGas c has been able to sell over 2500 units of biogas, which has improved the livelihoods of over 12,500 people in the region.

The market in Tanzania is not big enough to make the company scale and this is the rationale for regional expansion, with the hope of selling over 1 million units of biogas in Africa. Many impact investors are looking for cross-border transactions as they provide the required scale.

Another good example in the energy sector is M-Kopa, a startup that has been looking to provide poor households with clean energy solutions across East Africa. The founders of M-Kopa realized that the problem of low electricity access transcends borders, with a simple and single solutions likely to work in any market.

The company's model is firmly based on mobile money, where customers can buy home solar kits on credit and pay through their phones for up to a year. They have so far opened operations in Kenya, Tanzania and Uganda.

M-Kopa, which was founded in 2011, had by January 2018 signed up more than 600,000 homes to its solar power solution, and was adding up to 500 new homes daily. At the same time, it has employed hundreds across the region as sales and support agents, achieving its founders' goals of making money while making a lasting impact at the same time.

DFIs and NGOs Are Still the Dominant Investors

Development financial institutions (DFIs) still remain the biggest investors in the impact space in the African continent. This is expected to remain the case in the coming future as they have the mandate and the resources that is quite unmatched by other classes of investors.

The DFIs from Europe are the most active in the impact investing space in the continent with Norfund, IFU, Swedfund and FMO and Proparco taking the lion share of the investments opportunity in Africa. These European DFIs are looking at investing in businesses that increase the creation of jobs, boost economic growth in a sustainable manner and fight poverty and climate change.

In 2018, Proparco, the French DFI helped arrange financing of over €40 million to SCOUL, Uganda's third-largest sugar manufacturing company, to finance a new 26MW co-generation power plant. The plant will help the company to generate renewable energy from waste.

The power will be both for internal use as well as for sale to the national grid. This production of green electricity from biomass will directly contribute to the UN Sustainable Development Goal #7 (affordable and clean energy) in a country suffering from a low electrification rate. It will also help the company to reduce its carbon footprint, a concept that is just beginning to take root in Africa despite having been at the fore of green discussions in the Western world for years.

This investment marks Proparco's second operation with SCOUL after an initial US$23 million loan granted in 2012, which helped the sugar company increase its production capacity and expand its technical assistance to smallholder farmers. This testifies to Proparco long-term commitment to a company recognized for its environmental and social practices and to the development of agribusiness in Uganda.

Support Ecosystems Are Maturing

The marketplace for impact investing in the continent is improving at a lightening rate.

There have been various angel network establishments taking place, and more and more incubators and accelerators are being established every month by governments that are finally appreciating the role of impact investing in driving social economic growth.

Governments are also encouraging investors and social entrepreneurs by producing an enabling environment through policies and regulations that are more favorable to investment.

In Kenya, one of the most visible examples of such an initiative is Enterprise Kenya. This was started in 2015 with the goal of driving innovation, research and development in the Information Technology (IT) sector, which has emerged as a key jobs driver in the economy. The initiative will also help entrepreneurs gain access to capital and provide support to existing incubators.

It is hoped that Enterprise Kenya, as a national accelerator, will help to catalyze innovations that could form part of the pipeline for financers interested in the ICT center in Kenya.

The Enterprise Kenya initiative provides services that help to minimize the risk of establishing and scaling an ICT business in Kenya, which is a key factor for investors to consider in an industry that is characterized by more misses than hits when it comes to scaling up start-ups.

These accelerator and incubator programmes will therefore provide a crucial connection between financiers, regulators and standard developers in the market, which will help the businesses to achieve scale. The objective of the government of Kenya investing in this initiative is to have the Buy Kenya IT, Build Kenya IT, To Build Kenya agenda strengthened.

More and more African countries such as Rwanda, Ghana and Tanzania have similar initiatives in different sectors such as agriculture, manufacturing and fishing. I expect that more and more initiatives with similar characteristics will be initiated by various countries and governments will be able to put public money into such initiatives with the hope that some of the ideas that will be incubated and accelerated in such accelerators will attract impact investors who will help to scale the businesses with impact such as increased jobs, more tax revenues and better products produced.

We expect therefore to see more impact investors scouting for such initiatives and forming collaborations that will enable them to have access to the pipeline from such initiatives or investments.

Impact Investing Is Becoming More Evidence Based

More than ever, impact investors and social entrepreneurs need to demonstrate the impact that they expect to achieve in order to sustain the rapid growth of this industry. Providing clarity to funders helps in the evaluation of the deals to invest in as it provides possible valuable input into the nature and amount of impact that should be expected in the business.

The fact that the investors are looking beyond the proof of concept is also a way of minimizing their risk. In 2014, I was involved in proofing the concept for KickStart International in one of their social enterprises dedicated to lifting millions of people in Africa out of poverty quickly, cost-effectively and sustainably.

Kickstart is offering a solution that helps in the transition from rain-fed to irrigated agriculture, which has afforded millions of Africans an opportunity to participate in profitable agri-businesses. They have reached over 1.1 million people with a sale of over 300,000 water pumps, which has led to establishment of over 200,000 farming businesses.

Most of the achievements were a result of the enterprise selling the human pump across Africa. This has helped the farmers to make more money, and to pave a dignified, sustainable path out of poverty.

KickStart has made significant progress in providing to the masses one of the world's lowest-cost, most efficient, solar-powered irrigation pumps for small-scale farmers. The company is partnering with various organizations to enable it to see the new products coming to the market in 2018.

The Autodesk Foundation and Kenya Climate Innovation Center are some of the companies that are collaborating with Kickstart for financing as well as for the design optimization work. In addition, the company has partnered with technology providers who are providing encapsulated brushless DC motor pumps. The advantage for Kickstart is that it has demonstrated across Africa that they have the required core technology, manufacturing capabilities, and existing economy of scale to move a product to full scale.

These are some of the considerations that impact investors in recent times are looking at as evidence that these proposed investments will have financial and impact returns.

KickStart has a lot of experience working with small-scale farmers and the product suggested here is an addition to the existing products, which will help the farmers to upgrade their existing technology and hence is seen as a more successful product as opposed to a case where it will be an introduction of a totally new product to the market. This just builds the case for the commercial parameters for the investment and hence it becomes more attractive to impact investors.

It is evident that from the idea of this product the company has been able to attract different forms of financing, which demonstrates the future trends. To inform this research and development and incorporate farmer feedback at every stage, KickStart has continued deploying and tracking an earlier solar pump model among farmers in Kenya and the region.

These trials yield critical insight that was incorporated into the forthcoming solar pump prototype, which will be field tested in 2018. The pump is on track to meet the rigorous design criteria and retail for a significantly lower price than any solar-powered irrigation pump currently on the market in Africa. It will also be priced below the up-front cost of most fossil fuel-powered alternatives.

In parallel, KickStart has been working with additional partners to refine pay-as-you-go (PAYG) financing offerings for solar irrigation systems, to further ensure that even the poorest households can access and benefit from these cutting-edge technologies.

As a progression to the human pump, the company has developed a solar pump, which is helping small scale farmers who are more commercial and scaling to have a more advanced products to meet their irrigation needs. The product has the unique potential to harness three of Africa's most plentiful and underutilized resources: entrepreneurial individuals; renewable energy and water resources.

KickStart designs and disseminates the tools and knowledge farmers need to sever their reliance on increasingly unpredictable rains as well as grow more food, often with simple yet transformative irrigation methods. The ability to harvest and sell crops year-round, particularly in dry seasons when food is scarce and expensive, empowers rural families to break the vicious cycle of hunger and poverty.

SDGs as a Platform for Impact Investment

In September 2015, at the UN Sustainable Development Summit, The United Nations presented a set of sustainable development goals (SDGs) that were signed off by over 190 countries as the mechanism that will lead to a better world without leaving any countries behind.

The goals are universal and applicable to both the developed and developing countries. The 2030 Agenda, as it is known, is aimed at succeeding the millennium development goals (MDGs) that were effective until 2015. The MDGs consisted of eight goals whilst the SDGs include 17 goals. The major distinction between the SDG and the MDG era is that for the SDGs to be achieved, the role of the private sector is seen as paramount.

This was not the case for the MDGs and is probably the reason that many of the MDGs were a struggle to achieve. One way that the private sector is being engaged is through the financing of the SDGs. Also in 2015, the UN held its Third International Conference on Financing for Development in Addis Ababa, Ethiopia. Here, countries committed to a new outlook on how to finance sustainable development, drawing on lessons learnt from previous efforts following similar meetings Monterrey, Mexico in 2002 and in Doha, Qatar in 2008.

Given the close correlation between impact investing and SDGs, we shall look with bit of detail at the resolutions of the Addis Ababa meeting, which will effectively form the basis for cooperation between governments and impact investors in the next decade or so.

Key to the Addis Ababa declaration was the recognition that private business activity, investment and innovation are major drivers of productivity, inclusive economic growth and job creation. The governments present said that they would henceforth commit to ensuring that there is coherence between their policies or regulatory frameworks and those of the development partners. These partners, they said, would help in scaling up capacity-building at all levels, thus buttressing sustainable development and poverty eradication, through the identification of these investors as equal partners in the development process.

By building a stable and transparent investment climate, the participating countries stated in their declaration that they would be able to give an incentive to the private sector to undertake long-term commitment in economies that actually need the jobs and opportunities that impact investment brings. However, in order to do this, governments in Africa need to reassure investors that they will properly enforce contracts, respect the rights of businesses and protect them from predatory activities from public sector hawks.

The governments also recognise that there is room in the sustainable investment and development model for philanthropic donors who, as we saw in earlier chapters, have been emerging as a key source of capital for impact investors. In the end, the governments stated that they would lay emphasis on projects that have the greatest social impact on their societies, mainly in the area of job creation.

In light of the developments as stated above, impact investors are now evaluating businesses in terms of how well they will be able to deliver some of the targets that are stipulated under the SDGs. This will mean that SDGs will become more integrated to impact investing and hopefully this move will help in the achievement of the sustainable goals by 2030.

In the recent past, I have seen more and more social enterprises that are seeking financing and other support providing the impact expected based on the SDG frameworks.

The investment presentation decks are providing information on what SDGs are being addressed by the investment. This trend is expected to continue at least until 2030 when the SDGs are expected to be under implementation for investors and fund managers.

It is important for impact investors to take time to familiarize themselves with the SDGs since they present a possible framework for the impact measurement and driving the investee companies towards SDGs will mean that the funders will be contributing to the objective of a better world for all.

Many impact funds are evaluating their portfolio in terms of how it directly impacts on the targets of the SDGs. A good example is Liechtenstein Global Trust (LGT) Impact Ventures, a Zurich-based US$71 million impact fund, which recently mapped it portfolio to 16 out of the 17 SGDs. The fund targets investing in investments which provides both the financial returns as well as impact returns in the forms of social and environmental considerations.

The fund invests in scalable business models to improve access to services and products in areas such as education, health, agriculture, energy, and information and communication technologies. In Africa, for instance, a lot of funds have invested in Bridge International Academies, which is currently serving more than 100,000 pupils in more than 520 nursery and primary schools across Kenya, Uganda, Nigeria, Liberia and India and with a mission of "Knowledge for all." This investment is expected to educate over 10 million children across a dozen countries by 2025.

The model of Bridge is to provide low-cost tuition to students in Sub-Saharan Africa and India. Bridge as a Portfolio Company for LGT provides contributions to SDG #4 regarding quality education. Bridge has faced many challenges in the African continent, some of which have already been outlined in Chapter 4.

On the positive side of things, the company has been able to attract funding from tens of impact investors including IFC, Commonwealth Development Corporation (CDC), Department for International Development (DFID), Novastar, the Bill and Melinda Gates foundation, Kholsa Ventures and Omidyar Network, among others.

Compensation Based on Social Goals

Compensation of the fund managers is increasingly being based on the success of the fund managers.

Traditionally, this was based on financial returns but for impact investing this is being based on both the financial returns and—more importantly—the impacts. This is a shift that is expected to continue especially for the open fund models discussed under Chapter 6. In the traditional private equity model, the funds management has a management fee and additionally will receive a carry from the returns achieved by the fund.

The carry is as a result of the financial return target and not on the expected return, such as the job created by the investee companies, the livelihoods transformed, the number people with more access to products and so on.

Recently, more and more impact investors are starting to tie their own compensation to the social goals met by their investments, to ensure aligned incentives. Impact fund managers will in the future not be judged by the amount of financial return they make but rather on the impact. This will require good definition of the return parameters as we established on the chapter on impact measurement. This is why the theory of change will be important as a starting point to map the kind of the impact that an impact investor or a fund is looking at.

The impact parameter will need to be agreed on in advance and, based on the achievement, the compensation will be determined. Under the Kenya Climate Venture, the fund is aiming for various impact-related parameters, such as increases in agricultural yields, the number of tons of carbon mitigated, the number of green jobs created, the number of units of low-carbon sources of energy supplied and the number of people with access to clean drinking water.

These parameters will vary from one investment to another as well as from one fund to another.

The management of the fund and the investors need to agree on what is to be reported on as the impact of the contributions. Once this is agreed, a logical framework can be developed, and this will form the basis of the evaluation of managers.

The challenge with compensation based on impact performance is that it takes a couple of years before results are seen. According to my experience, it actually takes closer to three years before the evidence of the impact caused by investments can be measured.

In the private equity fund world, the General Partners (GPs) compensation is based on the financial performance of the fund, which is determined from a carry or carried interest, which is the percentage of the financial earnings of the fund. In the impact sector, the tendency has been to use financial returns as the basis of compensation. In the recent past, more and more impact funds are also considering the level of impact and have bonus schemes that are based on the impacts generated by the fund. A good example is Kenya Climate Ventures, which is now considering both the financial returns of the funds as well as the impacts related to climate change mitigation and adaptation as way of compensation for the investment management team.

Certification of Impact

Certification of impact is becoming important in the impact investment space. This is where the impact that the investee companies and, by extension, the investors are claiming are certified or assured in order to ensure that they reflect the actual achievements.

This is aimed at building confidence in the impact investing space and there has been a couple of organizations that are being involved in the certification for impact results. Others are proving measurement tools as well as reporting frameworks on how to report the impacts. This trend is heating up due to the need for confidence building and will be even more important in the future. This will improve the transparency of the work that the fund managers and the investee companies are doing. It will also be a useful choice of work for the High Net Worth Individuals (HNWI) foundation and other investors as they will be able to ascertain the claims of the fund managers.

The result of this movement is that more and more fund managers and investee companies are incorporating measurement tools and methodologies. These are led by monitoring and evaluation (M&E) experts who will start by providing the baseline on the investee companies at the various levels of a business growth pathway just before the investment is made and will continue monitoring and evaluating the results from the operational arm of the company with the hope that this will provide a good story for future funding.

The M&E team should be conversant with the investment processes to enable them to be involved on all the stages of investment, starting from pipeline determination to post-investment management to exits. At the approval stage, the investment evaluator will be looking at the possible impacts and incorporate the same to the investment approval papers for decisions. The team will also be establishing the baseline for each case and for the deal so that, at the presentation, the impact can be presented as the well as the baseline. In the future, they will monitor and support the investments with the hope that they will provide a financial return as well as an impact return.

Another role for the monitoring activity is to help the team and the fund manager to learn from both the strengths as well as the weaknesses to make the fund appropriate.

It is good practice to have the M&E team engaged on a day to day activities of the fund as this will be useful for the management of the fund who will use the resulting M&E data to manage the operations of the fund.

B-Corp Movement and Shift to Impactful CSR

B-Corps are for-profit companies certified by the nonprofit B-Lab to meet rigorous standards of social and environmental performance, accountability, and transparency. In 2018, there are more than 2100 Certified B-Corps from 50 countries and over 130 industries working together towards one unifying goal: to redefine success in business to mean the impact to society.

More and more impact investment companies are seeking certification as B-corporations. Being B-Corp essentially means that a company has demonstrated that it has impact, is legally accountable and that it has shown transparency in its dealing with the public and customers. This is being achieved with the collaboration of B-Labs, which are helping thousands of businesses, investors, and institutions measure and manage their impact. In addition to the movement to B-Lab, more and more companies are considering corporate sustainability (CS) as part of their DNA and many social enterprises are emerging form this movement.

There is move from companies in Africa engaging in the traditional CSR and this has resulted in the matters of sustainability being given priority in many businesses across the continent.

Businesses have traditionally not involved themselves in tackling the social challenges that countries face and, for a long period, this was seen as a role of government. Occasionally, a business, in very isolated cases, would involve itself in some sort of philanthropy trying to solve some of these problems.

The concern with the philanthropy perspective is that it was considered after the bottom line of the company and was also seen as an extra cost to the business at the expense of the shareholders. The solving of the social problems by business was seen to have direct implications for their economic results. The reason for this is that, traditionally, the role for business has been to maximize profits; for example, under neoclassical economics and several management theories, it has been assumed that the role of a business is to maximize economic gains for its shareholders.

Profit maximization relates to the shareholder's theory and is has been in existence for more than two centuries since it was proposed by Adam Smith as proposed in his book The Wealth of Nations. In 1970, Milton Friedman argued that the raison d'être for business was to ensure that the wealth of its stock holders is at the maximum.

In the recent past, the shareholder's theory has been replaced by the stakeholder's theory. The stakeholder's theory advocates other parties being involved in the business ecosystem which includes the likes of government, civil society and NGOs, trade unions, communities, financiers, general public, suppliers, employees and customers.

In this case, the shareholders are treated as the ultimate residual beneficiary since they are the provider's financial resources for the business. This has resulted in businesses moving CSR from the philanthropy perspective to a more integrated way.

For businesses to be able to address the stakeholder theory, there are a number of variables that businesses need to consider in terms of doing business and these include: the business also caring about other stakeholders in addition to shareholders, companies looking at their performance more from a long-term perspective as opposed to quarterly and semiannual performances; and focusing on the ethical grounds of their decisions.

SDGs, as noted earlier, are creating a platform that will help companies to move towards more coordinated CSR which is more relevant, and which is a win–win for all the parties involved.

Stakeholders who are individuals or groups that affect or could be affected by a firm's objectives becoming central to the interaction of business and society. The firm's responsibilities have moved beyond shareholders to stakeholders which means that for a firm to survive there is need to for dependency on stakeholders since stakeholders are the resource owners; both material or immaterial resources. The implication has been firms commitment to pro-social actions to maximize the value of the stakeholders by conforming to stakeholders norms and this has fueled impact investing even from the traditionalist businesses which did not consider the stakeholders other than shareholders in the past.

The move towards sustainability is expected to continue and will contribute to the impact investing sector in various ways. First, it will create more and more social enterprises, which will be spawn out of traditional business and hence the pipeline for investors will increase and the companies producing such enterprises will be the anchoring shareholders. Second, the movement will contribute to the private sector encouraging social entrepreneurship, as we have seen in the recent past.

Starting in Kenya, Safaricom, the leading mobile operator in East Africa has established a fund named Spark Fund.

Safaricom as a responsible business has evaluated its role in strengthening the start-up and impact sector in East Africa and as a result has come up with a blue print to help start-up businesses in the mobile sector. The support will be in the form of resources such as technology and financing, which will enable such ventures to achieve scale.

Safaricom is the leading mobile provider in East Africa and has established a venture fund that is capitalized to the tune of US$1 million for the purposes of investing in late seed to early growth stage companies in the field of mobile technology. The fund is seen as an enabler for start-ups in the sector that are aimed at enhancing the service delivery for the mobile telephone users in Kenya and the region. The fund will also provide the technical support as well as business development support, which will be leveraged on Safaricom's dominant and leading position in the mobile telephone sector in Africa.

The fund is aimed at taking monitory investment in business in the form of equity and mezzanine financing, which is convertible, and the average deal sizes so far has been in the range of US$60,000–220,000.

Considering that Safaricom does not have the expertise in impact investing, the company has collaborated with an impact fund from Kenya—TBL Invest—which will provide the required investment experience as well as sitting in the investment committee of the Spark Fund. These fund managers will be responsible for deal management as well as portfolio management.

In addition, the Safaricom business has been supporting enterprises through the in-kind support by providing free access to SMS USSD access, API's and integration services, cloud hosting and marketing opportunities, which all has resulted in better growth of the companies being supported by the Spark Fund.

The Rise of the Nonprofit Social Enterprise

In 2016, there was a change in the rules on the operation of the foundations in the USA, whereby they are required by law to distribute 5% of their assets every year to non-profits that are making a difference. This will mean that more and more funding from the foundation is going to nonprofit organizations.

Table 5.1 Kickstart international funding mix

SOURCE OF FUNDING	PERCENTAGE
Foundations	43%
Individuals	11%
Corporations	9%
Earned Income	36%
Governments	1%
Total	**100%**

Source KickStart International 2017 annual report

Due to this, more and more nonprofits organizations are now establishing social enterprises that are marketed as nonprofit. A good example of this is Kickstart International, which is an international nonprofit social enterprise.

This structure is helping the companies to attract funding that otherwise would not have been available. The funding for this structure is mainly from foundations and individuals. For instance, looking at Kickstart international annual report for 2017, it was clear that foundations still form the largest source of funding.

This is complemented by the revenues generated from other sources. In the case of KickStart, the funding from foundations was 36%, forming its second largest source of financing Table 5.1.

Impact Investing Is Becoming More Mainstream

In the recent past, there has been a more inclusivity in the impact investing sector. The traditional investors such as pension funds, foundations, commercial banks, sovereign funds are now focusing more on the impact investing sector.

There are various indicators that reflect the fact that impact investing is becoming mainstream, which includes the trillion of dollars being committed to impact investing.

There has been a significant move in business schools where more and more students are enrolling in impact investing classes rather than in the traditional investment classes. Another parameter is that more and more millennials and especially women are being interested not just in jobs for the sake of money but also for the impact they have, which has led to more interest in work with a purpose—the purpose being the impact on livelihoods.

The leading banks in impact investing in 2018 according to Euro money wealth management survey includes UBS; Credit Suisse, HSBC, BNP Paribas and JPMorgan.

Another recent mainstream entrant into impact investing is BlackRock where the top management of BlackRock, led by the founder and chief executive, Larry Fink, wrote to the CEO of the investee companies in BlackRock portfolio with investment totaling over US$6 trillion encouraging them to consider the societal implications of their business decisions. This is line with the move that society is demanding that companies, both public and private, serve a social purpose.

Blackrock is interested in the financial sustainability of its investments but, more importantly, is now becoming interested in the social and impact returns, which provides a good basis for the impact investing.

Companies—at least those in the portfolio of BlackRock—will start to move towards allocating more money to investments that will result in impact, which will provide a leverage for impact investing.

Foundations are also committing an even a greater percentage of their funds into impact investing; for example, Ford Foundation has stated that they will commit more than US$1 billion of its endowment to impact investing. This is a positive move because it will provide an example to other foundations to have their endowment invested in impact investing rather than money being put into the traditional program-related funds.

The existence of the SDGs and the need for the private sector to contribute to the achievement of the SDGs is also playing a role in having more mainstream investors taking up impact investing. SDGs acts as a focal point for mobilizing the private sector capital required to fund the development financing gap, which is estimated to be close to US$3 trillion.

Another reason that is making the traditional investors move toward impact investing is the fact that the impact sector is maturing, and hence more and more traditional investors are seeing potential for financial returns as well as the impact returns. It is expected that as the sector matures, more and more financiers will be attracted, hence making the sector even more traditional in terms of the funds under management. There has also been some democratizing of impact investing, which has provided more people with the opportunity for impact investing as well as increasing the resulting impacts. This has resulted in more and more individuals and organizations becoming more interested in impact investing

Market Data Will Be Key Going Forward

Far too often, the concept of impact investing leads to the misconception that the investors are just looking to do good and do not care about returns.

As we said in the introductory chapter, impact investing is not charity, and hence the 'social' aspect of the investment cannot be allowed to supersede the 'business' side.

Pioneer impact investors in Africa, and indeed any investor in Africa, initially entered into a greenfield market that had very little in the form of data or information that could be relied upon to guide investments. State data was also patchy, with many governments scoring poorly in terms of keeping up-to date national economic statistics. As we shall see in a case study in Chapter 8 of this book, going into a market without sufficient data and information can ruin an otherwise well thought out investment.

The demand for data by investors is, however, catalyzing a change in the way African governments and companies are collecting, treating and storing information. Many countries, including Kenya, have reinforced their national bureaus of statistics, and are now tracking their economic performance on many fronts.

Kenya for instance has been producing a detailed statistical abstract for more than a decade now, filling in information gaps that would otherwise have proven extremely expensive and time consuming for an investor to research. However, it must be said that this is still a work in progress, and there is room for improvement.

In addition to official data, the early-bird investors have also gained valuable information and collected vital data from the markets in which they operate.

This database built over the past decade or so is now becoming available to new market entrants, some of whom are also partnering with the older investors in impact investments. The rapid rise in the use of technology in Africa has also helped. For instance, a startup like M-Kopa receives a lot of data on its customers' financial habits, purchasing power and the like. This can be leveraged when they or their collaborators are looking to launch a new product in the market, informing decisions such as when or where to invest, and the type of product that would work with the target market.

Technology is also helping investors with tracking the impact of their investment. Gone are the days when the investor would need to hire a small army of workers to assess whether the investment is having an impact. Mobile-based surveys can now be deployed effectively to track impact, with the community giving constant feedback that is more nuanced than a blanket survey would ever have achieved. This data, as we have said above, is also easier to collate and store, keeping it ready for use by new investors. Therefore, the impact investor who can best harness this market data starts off at a distinct advantage compared with one who does not have access to it.

This becomes important when looking at the sustainability factor, which is a big problem in Africa where many start-ups fail primarily due to poor market research.

Conclusion

The trends we have looked at above are likely to remain in flux in line with a changing business environment. New trends are likely to appear in the next few years as the impact investment sector matures and grows to reach global standards and more funds flow into the continent.

Investors coming into Africa would therefore be well advised to keep their eyes on the market and ears to the ground in order to protect themselves from falling behind in the industry and losing money in their investment.

We have so far enumerated up to ten trends that are the most visible in the impact investing space in Africa. However, it is important to accept that we cannot fully exhaust the number of trends that will emerge, given that we are dealing with an extremely spontaneous market where opportunities crop up daily and existing ideas that seemed ironclad a few months ago suddenly lose their sheen.

It is important to keep in mind that Africa is growing more and more interconnected with the spread of technology—internet, telecommunications and even electricity connection that buttresses this technology. This has made it necessary for businesses to look outside their borders in order to achieve scale, something that we have seen with the likes of M-Kopa.

It has also helped that support ecosystems are maturing, and businesses are able now to count more on policy makers to help them gain a foothold with better and clearer tax regimes, better legal protection of contracts and other enablers like cheaper power and better transport links.

It is interesting that DFIs still remain the biggest investors in the impact space in the African continent, leveraging on their resources that are quite unmatched by other classes of investors and longer experience on the ground.

This, in my view, represents both a challenge and an opportunity for new investors. A challenge because, in chasing deals, it may be impossible to compete with these behemoths, and an opportunity because in their many years here they have in some ways prepared the ground for new investors. Many of the challenges new investors would have faced, such as regulatory issues, they faced a long time ago, and probably have lobbied hard with government to have them removed. It is also possible for new investors to borrow from the experiences of these institutions to avoid making mistakes as they foray into a new environment.

As impact investing comes of age, however, investors need to provide evidence that their investment is having the impact expected in order to sustain the rapid growth of this industry. In this regard, we expect that impact investors will align their objectives with those of the SDGs of the UN, which provide a measurable template which to judge your impact.

In the same vein, it is therefore expected that impact investors will refine and look to standardize their impact measurement tools, which at present are very varied.

At the end of the chapter, we have also noted the important role that collection and analysis of data will play in the industry going forward. This data will inform the choices of anyone looking to launch a new product in the market, when or where to invest, the type of product that would work with the target market. In short, it will be the determinant of the future success of impact investing.

As we shall see in the next two chapters, information and proper market intelligence form a key part of designing a fund. In short, setting up a fund without having all the relevant information available about the target market is inadvisable and may lead to failure.

6

Structuring a Fund

This chapter will look into how to go about impact investing as well as how to structure a fund.

When an investor is looking for a fund manager or an investment vehicle in which to invest, it is critical that a rigorous selection process be carried out as it forms a key success factor for any impact investment interventions. This process is underpinned by a far-reaching pipeline development process, which involves identifying the most promising entrepreneurs and business models, whilst understanding the growth potential of the markets in which they operate. Before approaching an investment, an impact investor ought to ensure that their strategies leverage their core competencies—in short, play to their strengths.

They should also understand the size of the opportunity they are pursuing (i.e., carry out market sizing) in order to avoid disappointment later when they realise the size of returns is not meeting expectations, or that they cannot fulfil the needs of the market within their scope of investment.

The investor should also seek to understand their market segments and the size of the opportunity in each market segments. This will then provide a solid basis for their growth assumptions and business valuation. It is also important to have accurate financial reports of a company prior to making an investment in it. Many investors have been led down a blind alley by unscrupulous investees whose only aim was to lay their hands on the capital.

This may require, as we discuss in Chapter 2, seeking legal advice and enlisting the services of a reputable auditor to carry out the business assessment and due diligence before committing funds.

© The Author(s) 2018
E. Mungai, *Impact Investing in Africa*,
https://doi.org/10.1007/978-3-030-00428-6_6

A company that has clean books will always be open to scrutiny by an investor, so watch out for signs of obstruction when seeking to look at the books of accounts. An investor should also be passionate about the opportunity they are pursuing but at the same time should make sure that they remain objective to the transaction.

One of the better tests of the seriousness of an investee should be in how much of their own capital they are willing to put into their own business. A serious entrepreneur should have a significant equity stake and not be an employee of some indifferent high-net-worth individuals who are angel investors.

Before and after the investment, it is critical that the investor looks into the strength of the governance, financial reporting, internal controls and regulatory compliance of the investee firm. The aim should be to look into the ways on how to align the organization's structure with the strategy and how to invest in building a winning investment in terms of impacts as well as financial returns. Sometimes it becomes necessary to mirror the corporate governance standards of an investee with those of the investor, especially in very young startups.

Mentorship will also be necessary in cases where the investor will need to help build the capacity of the investee company and the entrepreneur to build and an inclusive leadership style and be willing to build a performance-based culture. The investor must also be willing to invest in capacity to monitor the portfolio, otherwise they will run the risk of losing oversight over whether the investments are having the desired impacts. The whole objective of the impact investing endeavour is to generate a return from the invested businesses in the form of impacts as well as recovering the capital that was invested into the business.

As we shall see in this chapter, oversight and measurement of impact should not be seen as an optional activity but rather should be taken to be a core aspect of impact investing. To be able to increase the value of the investments, there is a need to consider the technical assistance (TA) facility and experience in managing this is also important. As an example, while establishing the Kenya Climate Venture (KCV)—a Kenya Climate Innovation Center (KCIC) with the funding from the World Bank—we had to ensure that there was a TA facility that would help to grow the companies with the hope of increasing the impacts as well as the financial returns. More on KCV will be covered on this chapter.

KCV management will identify the managerial support that each business requires in order to enhance its ability to scale, and the capacity of its founder and his/her team to manage the resultant growth.

Effective mentors and business advisors will be brought into the picture, trusted to be able to add true value to the KCV investees' management teams and to the business. To be able to identify the needs of the company, it is a requirement that the team involved have experience in early-stage financing and structuring such transactions, as well as identifying and managing the TA needs over the period of the investment.

These skills should be ensured at the level of the chief investment officer and investment managers of the fund under question and this will form one of the key success factors for the fund to translate the investments into a success. As the fund achieves scale, it is important, to get into partnerships with other parties and especially investors and other financers in order to secure co-investment and follow-on investment for the investees. If funds from partners, such as pension funds and commercial investors are being relied upon to scale the investment, it is necessary that the fund has a healthy pipeline that will be open for future investments and to scale up as the size of the fund grows.

Partnerships with like-minded investors in Africa are always an advantage since it allows investors to tap into a rich pool of information and experience especially when going into countries where the investors limited experience.

As the process of making investment progresses, it is important both at the individual investee companies as well as a fund to consider the exits options that are available to the investor. This is an often overlooked, but critically important aspect to consider when making investments in the African continent. It is essential for investors to think ahead to an exit mechanism when investing in Africa.

The African continent, unfortunately, lacks to a large extent sufficient home-grown capital to take over businesses when foreign investors are looking to make an exit. In Europe and the USA, for instance, exits are made easier by the existence of large, vibrant stock markets where one can take their business public.

There are also enough high-net-worth investors, companies and funds who can afford to buy out a business, especially one that is doing well. It is quite the opposite situation in Africa, and an investor needs to know that before choosing where and in what to invest in. Only a handful of African stock markets have capacity worth mentioning, and even they, by global standards, are considered really small.

One of the options that is more readily available is to sell investment to private equity funds. These funds, in the recent past, have shown increasing appetite for African investments as they chase returns from fast-growing economies. However, many will tend to show an appetite for young businesses, looking to grow them and then sell them off after 7–10 years.

Thus, investors run the risk of finding that private equity funds are too similar to some impact investors when it comes to investment horizon.

The choice of investment also matters when making an exit. Some of the 'hot' investment areas, such as agribusiness, education, healthcare, financial services and fast-moving consumer goods (FMCG) are easier to exit, because they will always have a ready taker nearby.

An investor should also keep an eye out for regulations on capital movement, availability of forex and taxation regimes. Some countries in Africa, such as Tanzania, and lately Nigeria, place a restriction on the amount of foreign exchange one can ship out.

This can leave an investor unable to transfer their capital out of the country after making an exit, which would essentially mean that it was not possible to invest it elsewhere. There are also some instances of countries running low on foreign exchange, bringing into place these restrictions. As explained in Chapter 2, regulations differ from country to country.

Going back to the topic of design funds, in 2016, while at KCIC, one of my main tasks was to establish an early-stage impact fund that was focused on climate investments. The initial seeding of the fund came from the World Bank, which had received close to US$5 million from the Danish and UK governments to establish a climate investment fund in Kenya.

The fund was to invest in clean-tech business both for returns and for the impact. The impact in this case was the reduction of carbon emissions, as well as helping Kenya to become more resilient to the effects of climate change. To establish the fund, KCIC hired the services of Carbon Trust UK who provided the advice on how to structure the fund. There were many lessons from the work of Carbon Trust and it is useful to share some of the findings here for those who are interested in establishing an investment vehicle in the impact space.

The fund structure can either be evergreen or a closed fund. One also needs to consider the governance structure of the funds as well as the make-up of the investment team. As such, this chapter will limit itself to issues of the fund structure, the management team, the skills required for impact investing and the governance structure that is optimal for such a fund.

Fund Structure

For impact investments, there is nothing like the one-size-fits all model, as prescribed by traditional investments. This will be determined by the circumstances of the investors and their investment thesis as well as the location in which they are considering making investments.

The fund structure is also driven by the future need for more investors in the fund as well as the exit mechanisms that will be available. Another determinant of the structure of the fund will be the nature and stage of the businesses in which the funds will be investing.

There will be need for flexibility from the traditional investment mechanisms to be able to accommodate the unique elements of the impact investing space. Under impact investing, the relationship between the impact investor and the entrepreneur needs to be excellent if the investment is going to succeed.

The traditional investment structures sometimes do not allow for this flexibility as it requires significant efforts to hand-hold the businesses. This calls for a huge contribution of time, resources and experiences from the investor in order to achieve success.

Businesses will go through various stages of growth, as we see in the diagram below. When structuring a fund, it is important to identify the stage at which you are entering the business, which as we shall see later in this chapter, influences the financing tools to be deployed (Fig. 6.1).

It is important that the investment structure be as simple and flexible as possible at the beginning and that it is built as the fund matures. This will ensure that the structure is left flexible with the hope that future investors will be able to fit in the existing structure and, if this is not possible, the changeover to meet the need of the future investors should be less painful. The structure of the fund in the recent past is seen to depend largely on the funders, both existing and potential, and their requirements.

When the funders are well defined, which is sometimes not the case, managers can develop an effective closed-fund structure. In the cases where this is not as well defined and where the fund is expected to continue raising funds, it is better to leave it as simple as possible and with more flexibility.

The trend is that more and more funds are going for the open-ended fund (e.g., evergreen funds where the preferred setup is that of an investment company). The reason for this is the attractiveness to investors, especially DFIs, who are willing to pay taxes and do not have a specified period by which they should divest their funds.

The fund structure may evolve over time depending on a range of factors including the needs of the new investors and the size of the fund as well as change of the investment thesis of the fund. In the recent past, we have seen funds that are being registered as companies limited by shares, which has provided a lot of flexibility although it is not that efficient from the tax perspective.

Another key assumption made on this kind of a structure is the fact that an investment vehicle is more an operating entity that will directly employ

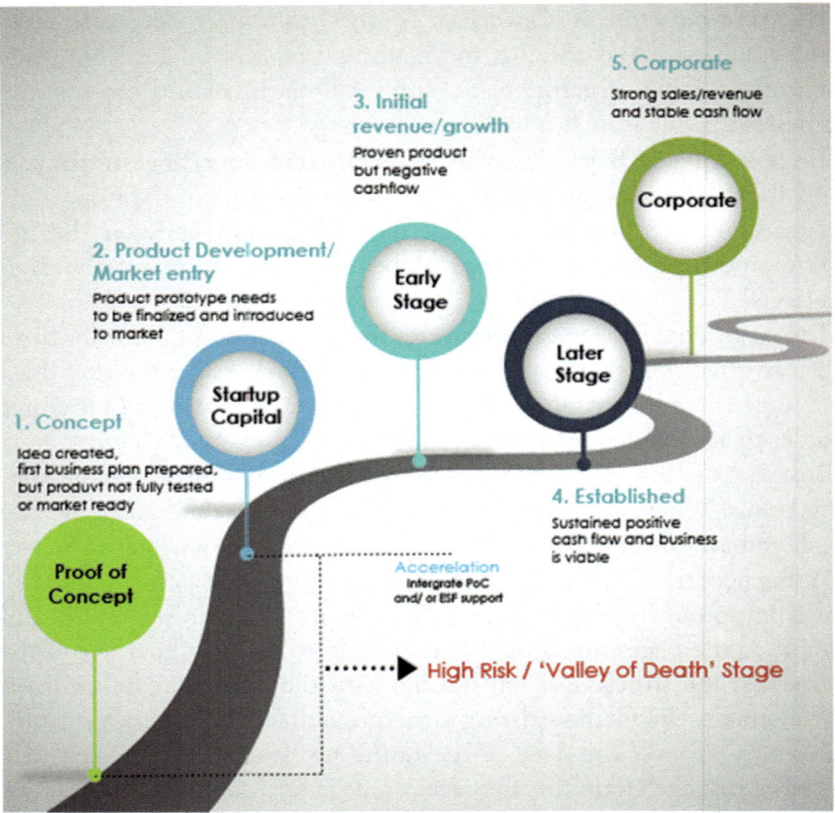

Fig. 6.1 Business growth stage and the required type of financing

the investment team as well as investing the funds that will be part of its balance sheet as opposed to an investment holding company where the investments are held in an offshore company.

The more flexible structure could only make sense at the start of the fund because soon after the investors are identified and the funds are committed, there will be need to produce the most effective and efficient structure for the fund.

That means that the initial structure of any fund could require some restructuring of the fund at the next phase and this is something the investors should bear in mind, especially in situations where they expect other investors to join into the fund as investors.

In the case of KCV, the initial phase was to have the fund as a company listed by shares—sort of an investment company that would then be transitioned to a more structured fund once the second phase financier of the fund was identified. This meant moving the fund from a more operational structure to a more investment-based structure. This called for considerations of the traditional private equity model and the possibility of being registered offshore.

Most of the funds in Africa are either registered in Luxembourg or Mauritius due to the favorable tax regimes there, in addition to the fact that these two destinations have proper ecosystems in place for the administration of funds, including lawyers, accountants, auditors, custodians and administrators.

The nature of the fund structure and its jurisdiction should be determined by the investors so as to make it attractive as possible for the liquidation as well as taxation perspectives. It is therefore imperative that fund managers should engage with potential investors on the structure and the registration structure of the proposed fund.

In terms of structure the funds, typically there will be three to four organs that form the governance and management of the fund. This will be the board or the board of advisers. This will depend on how the fund is registered, second, there will be the investment committee (IC) of the fund, which will be charged with the evaluation of the transactions as well as the evaluation of the post-investments management. The third organ is the management of the fund, which is the day-to-day manager of the fund and, finally, depending on the size as well as whether there is funding for TA, there will be a TA committee, which will be in charge of the decisions as well as the monitoring of the TA funds.

Each of these organs is discussed below as they form a good part of the due diligence assessment for the potential investors as they drive the success of the fund, among other factors (Fig. 6.2).

Board of Advisers (Company Board)

Depending on how the fund is registered, there will be a need for a board of advisers or a board of directors. For instance, in the case where the fund has taken the shape of the permanent capital structure and hence registered as a company limited by shares, there will be need, as per the requirements of the law in many countries in Africa, to have an official board of directors who have the fiduciary duties.

On the other hand, if there is no such a structure, the board of advisers will be in place and the members of such a board will not have the fiduciary duty to the fund and in most cases will be representing the interests of the

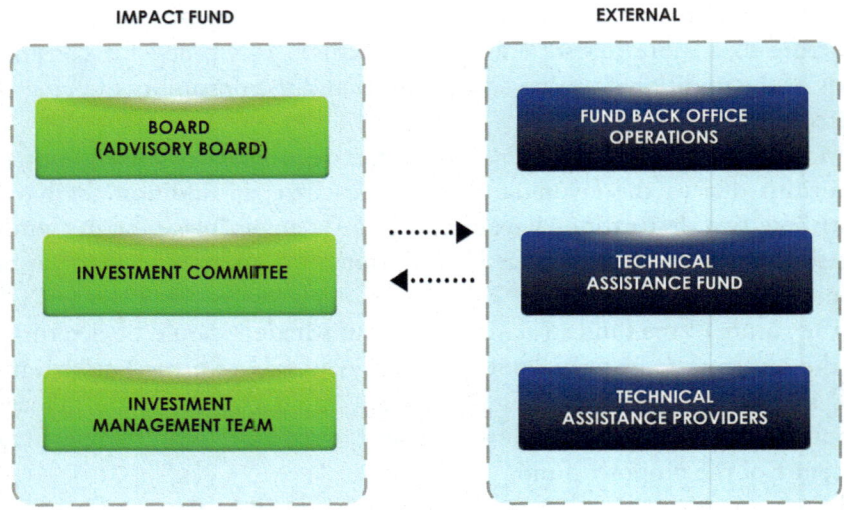

Fig. 6.2 A typical governance structure of impact fund

investors in the fund. For the purposes of the discussions on this section, the importance of the board of advisers and that of the board of directors is the same.

The board have an oversight responsibility to ensure that the fund is managed in the best interest of the investors. The board will consist of investors and other independent parties who will have had some previous experience on the governance of funds as well as impact investing and in Africa.

The board will ensure compliance of the fund with all the regulations, proper reporting and proper management of any conflict of interest as well as providing the overall strategy of the fund.

The optimum board size is seven members and all members should have one voting right. Seven is the optimal number of board members but depending on the size of the fund this could be reduced to five. The knowledge and experience of the board should be broad in order to ensure value addition.

The board members should have the requisite experience and competencies to deliver effectively on their role. The investors should ensure that the board is made up of people of high repute and integrity and who have the relevant experience. This will be a key factor in the additionality of the board as well as for the purpose of fund raising if the fund will need to raise funds at a later stage. Many investors will consider the profile of the board members to ensure that their funds are in good and experienced hands.

Investment Committee

The IC of the fund has one of the most critical roles in ensuring that the objectives of the investor are met. This is the think tank and the decision making organ on matters of investments to be made by the funds and how those transactions should be structured and be managed over the period of investment.

Its members ensure that capital is deployed as per the laid-out criteria and that they make sense for the fund and that the investee companies will be able to return the money as well as make an impact. The management team provide proposals for investment consideration to the committee who will use their judgement to decide which investments will be worthwhile for the fund.

It is important to ensure that the IC is independent from the management of the fund. In cases where it is a permanent structure and the fund is registered as an investment management company, there will be need for the IC to be recognised as a committee of the board of the fund. In any case, the decision of the IC will only be ratified by the board.

The IC members will need to have the experience in impact funds and will be expected to advise the management of the best way to select, carry out due diligence as well as manage the investments, including the provision of the TA. Ideally, they need a track record in impact investing/venture capital/private equity in the Africa, operational experience in building and scaling early-stage businesses with a deep appreciation of the local business environment, and a technical and practical knowledge of the sectors targeted by the fund.

The IC is responsible for approving, managing and exiting from investments. This means that the committee is involved in overseeing all the investment and programmatic activities of the impact fund including monitoring the investment pipeline and providing guidance to management as needed on how to develop and screen the pipeline; reviewing and approving the terms, timelines and TA budgets for individual investment opportunities; and monitoring the investment including approving any changes in the portfolio.

For a fund to be a success, the IC has also to have 'local knowledge,' given that most investees in Africa will not really fall in line with traditional Western principles where a business can be evaluated based on the excellence of its PowerPoint presentations and Excel sheets. The input from the IC on the market, the business model, the product, the technology and the entrepreneurs will be key to making the investments a success.

The Fund Management Team

The investment team is a critical success factor that the investor should focus on. There is need to build a qualified and experienced team to manage the investments. It is worth noting that the impact investment team will require special skills compared with their counterparts who manage private equity funds.

The skills will need to include monitoring and evaluation skills, impact measurement and identification skills as well as the traditional investment skills. In most cases, the deals relate to small- and medium-sized enterprises (SMEs), which are a different kind of animal compared with large organizations.

For instance, a higher level of patience is needed when investing in an SME compared with a large organization, with losses early on being a very real possibility because the smaller businesses traditionally find it harder to compete in African markets.

The investment management team will also require the skills to manage TA funds since there will be need for such funds to make the investment cases a success. Experience will also be useful, more so in popular impact sectors such as agriculture, renewable energy—basically those sectors at the bottom of the pyramid section of the market. Most of the work of the investment management team will require a lot of hand holding.

The investment structuring experience in the impact sector is also key to enabling the team to manage the investments, as well as for the purposes of the exits from the fund. In addition to the deal management skills, there is need for the vehicle to have some capacity to undertake the back-office work, which will include communication, accounting work, impact measurement and administration of the investments. In some cases, especially in the initial phases of the fund, these efforts or skills could be outsourced from third parties for the purposes of efficiency. Other than the investment skills, it is important that the team has fundraising skills.

Fundraising can be done internally or can be outsourced but with the investment team in charge to ensure that the narrative and the promises that are being made by the third-party fundraiser are compliant with the mission and the vision of the fund, especially in regard to the expected impact. In the initial phases of the fund, when the team is likely to be small, some level of specialization is required when choosing the sectors in which to invest.

While big impact funds can afford to look at a number of sectors, since they have the bandwidth to do so, new funds that are limited by team size might find it more prudent to begin with a specialization on a certain sector. This will enable the team to harness deep experience on one sector before branching out to another sector. This enhances the likelihood of success. As the team grows and as the capacity is built within the fund, there will be a possibility of expanding to more sectors. The fund will therefore need to have an IC, as that will guide the wider team from an investment perspective.

As noted above, it will be critical that the founders of the impact fund ensure that the members of the IC have the relevant skills and that will be able to take on a more enhanced role. They should support the investment team but at the same time ensure that their independence is maintained in accordance with the governance requirement of the fund.

The IC can help to bridge the gap in experience of the team in a more advisory role as opposed to replacing the investment team role. In addition to having the IC, the fund can outsource the services of experts in the different sectors in which it is investing. This will come in useful when it comes to the provision of the TA as well as the evaluation of the business case of the investment and how this can be improved.

The fund should also borrow from the experience of other funds and seek co-investment with such funds. This will act as a bridge of knowledge and also improve the efficiency in managing the deal as well as carrying out due diligence. It is said that two eyes are better than one and hence co-investment could also be a good option, particularly for new funds with new investment teams until they have gained enough experience.

The fund's management should scale as the fund size grows in the form of funds under management. The ideal parameter to check the adequacy of the funds team is the number of investments managed by one investment manager. Typically, the ideal number for this is three investments. Three is the magic number, considering the fact that in impact investing, the role of the investment officer is that of hand-holding the entrepreneur.

Therefore, to have the bandwidth and the time, there is a need to limit the number of investment that each investment manager is responsible for. It should be noted that this is one of the biggest challenges in the impact investing.

We have seen managers managing more than six investments and the results in terms of impacts and financial returns is evident as the manager does not allocate enough time to each investment to be able to add value.

Under impact investing, there is need to have a balance in the level of sophistication in deal making and the hunger to do the deal.

The management of the fund will be the one to determine which investment makes the cut and can be presented to the IC.

This is why the experiences highlighted above are important—to ensure that the management of the fund is able to access the right deals and ask for the right information.

For instance, one fund operating in the East Africa region looked at 240 enterprises in 2016, and only invested in two. This is due to the rigor of the investment team, which unfortunately was made up of bankers who looked for perfect Excel models, good PowerPoint pitch decks and audited financials from one of the top accountants and well-articulated business strategies. This is not what impact investing is about. Impact investing is about looking at the entrepreneurs and having the conviction that they can do the job; it is looking at the products and the potential market.

Once these entrepreneurship team; product(s) and potential market are in place, the next step is for the investor to consider an investment and handhold the entrepreneurs, not as an investor but as a business partner.

Investments in the impact sector are not a science but an art and hence will require the consideration of the investee companies and the entrepreneurs, both from the perspective of their business acumen and their knowledge. In most cases, this knowledge is not there but nevertheless the investee companies have the conviction and the passion to grow their businesses.

To illustrate the point regarding knowledge, one of the impact funds operating in Kenya carried out due diligence on an agricultural case and they were satisfied that the case was a good one for investment and presented it all the way to their IC with positive news. They prepared a term sheet for the investment, which was shy of 54 pages with more than 24 conditions precedent.

The entrepreneur in question was not sophisticated and did not have any university education or knowledge in finance and hence the term-sheet was like rocket science to her. However, only few clauses on the terms sheet mattered to her: how much she was getting in investment and the terms of the investments. In this case, the loan was to be in US dollars and was for five years with a grace period of six months.

The business was exporting produce to Europe and was based in Kenya and yet the investment team at the impact fund deemed it fit to provide a dollar loan. On the basis of this clause, the entrepreneur declined the US$2 million loan from the impact fund; she was unable to understand clauses such as drag along, exit multiples and so on, which really did not make sense for the entrepreneur and her final choice was to stay away from the deal.

The good news is that the entrepreneur secured an equity investment from another fund who treated her not like an investee per se, but as a partner. This investor had confidence in the transaction and the entrepreneur even though her business did not have an accounting department and the audited accounts were not from one of the big accounting firms.

However, because the entrepreneur, the products and the market ticked the right boxes, the new investor saw a good deal, and went ahead to provide TA to the entrepreneur to grow the businesses. The business now has an outgrower group of over 2500 households in rural Kenya.

The Investment Approach

There is need to have a rigorous process in place to select the pipeline on one hand and flexible mechanisms on the other hand, in order to decide what businesses makes sense for any fund. Pipeline generation is still one of the key success factors and fund managers should be able to identity the best opportunities that should be considered for investment.

There is a need, therefore, for an efficient, responsive investment process from pipeline generation through to deal execution in order for an investor to be successful, with proper risk management in place. Investors may want to consider due diligence, portfolio diversification, product mix offering, valuation, dilution, liquidation, and credit and collateral risks while undertaking an investment.

The investment process under impact investing will mainly comprise of the four stages illustrated (Fig. 6.3).

Deal Origination

The deal origination will involve the identification of possible deals and deal evaluation and screening of the investments to determine what will form the pipeline for the investor.

Within deal origination, especially for impact investing, it is important that the investors are able to innovate, especially in determining how efficiently they screen and select investments, and thereafter close the transaction to keep costs at a manageable level for small-sized deals.

In addition, the structures that they adopt for the new investments need to be well defined and thought out, given the higher risks associated with impact investing in start-ups and early-stage companies.

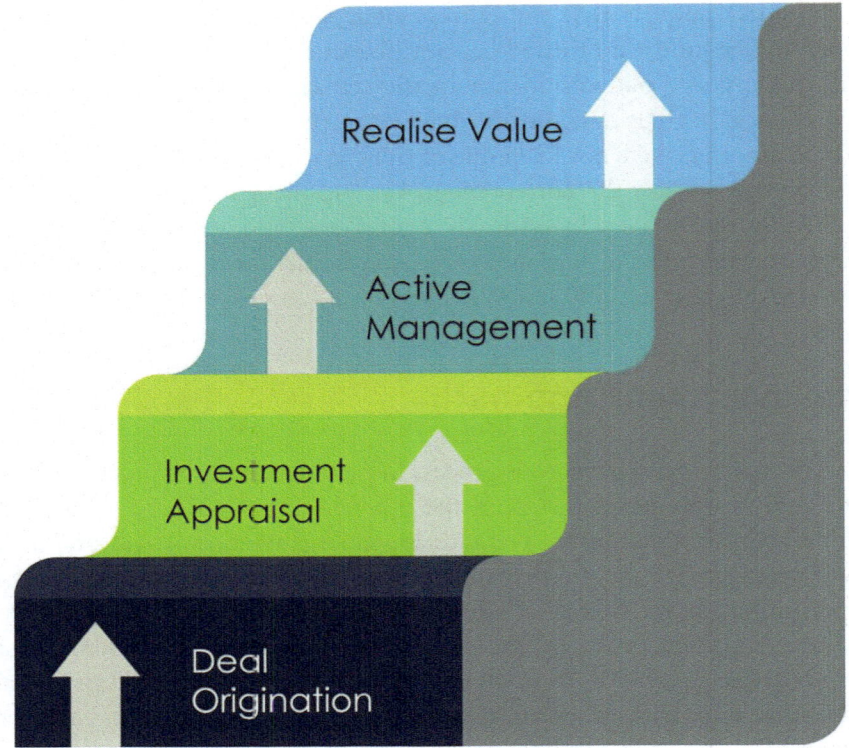

Fig. 6.3 Investment origination and management stages

As one evaluates the deals, it is also critical to consider the issue of exit. The investor will be faced with the question of how to achieve the exit, given that the traditional exit routes (e.g., sale to industry investor, put option or listing) are unlikely to be viable in most cases.

General Pipeline Considerations

Identifying a pipeline of viable investee companies is crucial for the success of investment efforts in Africa, where information on firms is hard to come by and many industries are still at their nascent growth stages.

There are a number of funds that are already present in Africa and hence the competition for suitable deals is high. The need to create such a pipeline means that the investment team is required to develop a close relationship with the community of investors and potential investee companies, especially with regard to the focus area of the specific fund.

There are two main ways for generating a deal pipeline. One is to have a close relationship with the players in the ecosystem in order to get referrals. The second is to have an application process whereby interested investee companies put in an application for funding for consideration by the investors.

Some of the possible deal sources for impact investors will include incubators and accelerators. In other cases, this will also be from organized hackathon challenges and boot camps as well as from competitions. In recent times, competitions have emerged as one of the major source of deals for impact investors.

For instance, incubator and accelerator programmes will run competitions where they will identify winners to be incubated or accelerated for a couple of months. As they become incubated, one of the major services that is provided to them is investor readiness, where the business models and products are refined to attract investors.

One way to capitalize on the deal flow is for the impact investors to collaborate, partner or even own incubator and accelerator programs that will feed the investment firms with the pipeline. For instance, at Kenya Climate Innovations Centre, we have, in the last six years, seen private investors investing close to US$20 million in incubated business.

Some of the examples of businesses coming out of the incubation programs include the likes of Angaza Design and Twiga Foods which are commanding huge fundraising rounds. In 2015, as I was involved as a judge under the 1776 competition in East Africa where Twiga Foods was picked as one of the winners. 1776 is a start-up incubator founded in Washington, DC by entrepreneurs Evan Burfield and Donna Harris in 2013 as a public-benefit corporation focused on solving societal challenges in regulated sectors such as education, energy, transportation and healthcare and has been running global entrepreneurship competitions.

Twiga identified a gap in the supply chain of fresh farm produce, mainly bananas, leveraging on technology to aggregate demand and link buyers to suppliers in Kenya's often fragmented agriculture markets.

The start-up, which was launched in late 2013, also offers credit lines to some of its vendor customers, ensuring that they are able to maintain a steady supply of produce and in effect keep prices stable and predictable.

To date, Twiga has been able to raise millions of dollars in funds from investors to grow its business. At the Kenya Climate Innovation Centre, the incubation centre provides a deals pipeline to the KCV—a fund that provides finance for climate-related investment with deal sizes up to US$500,000.

There is a possibility for economies of scale and exclusivity for a deal when this model is adopted. In addition, the cost of due diligence is significantly reduced given that the deals are already known within the group and hence not much due diligence is required at the appraisal stage. It is critical, therefore, that the impact investor builds a good reputation since this has a positive and direct relationship with the capability of deal sourcing. There is therefore a need for a strong brand, as well as for leveraging its relationship with other stakeholders and partners in the market to attract good pipeline deals.

The networking ability of the investor is also an important driver of the quality of the deals sourced and there is a need for the investor management, board members and the IC members to invest in personal and professional networks to the greatest extent possible, as this will bring them in contact will possible deals and hence expand their reach with regard to deals.

The deal screening should be based on a simplified evaluation criterion, which will enable the investor to quickly determine which deals makes sense to move to the next stage of the deal implementation cycle. The criteria mainly include aspects such as sector fit, impacts expected, geographical location fit, the stage of the business on the business development cycle and so on.

The outcome at this stage should always be a clearance in principle (CIP) and, depending on the governance structure of the investors, this could be provided by the IC. This will mean that the IC has provided the go-ahead to management to look further to the cases approved and possibly incur resources to conduct thorough due diligence.

Once the approval is provided, the deal goes to the second development stage: the deal appraisal.

The rule of the thumb from my experience is that one will require close to 100 possible cases to be able to arrive at a shortlist of about five companies that should be moved into the appraisal stage. This is a significant number and it shows why the success of the investing in impact investing will depend on how well the investors are able to generate possible pipeline companies. This is even more complicated in the instances where there are many impact investors scouting for deals. A possible solution for this challenge for investors will be looking at deal sourcing as a strategic issue and having a vehicle that is able to deliver deals on an exclusive basis.

The drawback with the model is that there will be a very high rejection rate from the program associated with the investors and hence there will be need for the investor to look into ways for mitigating this risk.

Investment Appraisal

At the investment appraisal stage, the investor will get into the analysis of the deal to ensure that it is a viable investment option.

We shall dwell at length on this stage, given its importance in realising success or failure for an impact investment fund.

The investee selection process will primarily be based on the target criteria framework in order to select the enterprises that will provide the maximum impact returns. Investors will be required to have a rigorous investment appraisal process.

First and foremost, investors need to ensure that they have the required deep understanding of the proposed case for investment and that they have a specific market niche that the investee is focused on and that it is at the right position on the industry value chain.

It is also important to ensure that the business is well positioned to capitalize on the opportunity in its chosen market segment. Investors need to appraise the entrepreneur and his management team, understand the industry, the target consumers and the geographical consideration of the area or country in which the investment is to be implemented.

As the business is evaluated, the investor will at the same time be able to identify the weak points of the specific business and devise ways on how to improve upon such weakness.

This will be more relevant in the cases where the investor has TA money that can be used to improve business operations. Co-investment with like-minded impact investors is worth considering as it provides a second opinion for the deals as well as cutting down on the due diligence costs and time since this is shared between the investors.

This will be a more appropriate strategy for those getting into the impact investing space for the first time or those who have limited experience. The additionality of the co-investment and follow-on investor will be the sharing of their prior knowledge of impact investing. This collaboration will be carried out in a cost-effective manner.

Another way to tap into the knowledge and experiences is to have an informal 'panel' of 3–5 experienced practitioners in the impact investment space who can periodically be providing insights into the target investee companies with the investors team during the screening stage, in order to get their views on the suitability or otherwise of a proposed investment.

Investment appraisal is a critical stage in the deal value chain as it is the stage where many things can go wrong in terms of investing in businesses that do not meet the criteria for investment. Investment appraisal will also provide insights in terms of the TA requirements as well as the structure of the deal and how the funds should flow into the investee company.

Investment Criteria

When carrying out the investment evaluation, there are a couple of elements that need to be addressed.

It is necessary to have investment filters that will vary from investor to investor. The potential deals should be subjected to the filters in order to ensure that the deals that the investors are considering meet the basic requirement of the fund or of the investor. While making an impact investment, it is important to take time to consider the proper criteria by which potential deals in the pipeline will be evaluated.

This will mean that the investors will need to define the key parameters that will help determine which companies should be progressed from pipeline to more readily investable cases which is higher of the on investment value chain.

The criteria should primarily be based on commercial parameters and impact parameters, as well as management-related parameters.

Commercial Parameters

Remember that the aim of the investor is to get a return from their investment even as they look to impact society positively. Most of the impact investors will be sector agonistic and will be looking at specific business proposals from such sectors as agriculture, energy, consumer products and so on.

It will be imperative for the investor to consider whether the proposed case fits within the specific sector. The investment size is normally given as a range. Most of the investors will specify the amount that can be invested in the transactions (deals ticket size that they are interested in).

This will therefore be a criterion for progressing the deals to the next level. Most of the impact investors in the continent claim to be interested in deals ranging from US$100,000–US$1.5 million. However, the investment need of the investee company is what guides the investor on whether the case is interesting for a particular fund.

The business will also need to demonstrate the potential to scale significantly, as defined by the identification of credible distribution partners and suitable supply chain infrastructure to enable initial service delivery and market penetration at an appreciable pace. In addition, the investee companies must be addressing a market of sufficient size at the price point contemplated, so that the business is able to make money.

The business should ideally have a source of sustainable competitive advantage that allows it to continue to grow, or to be an attractive acquisition target over time. This sustainable competitive advantage could come from intellectual property protection, including patents (which may be pending) from a more efficient business model, or processes from a fundamentally lower-cost product architecture, or from another key differentiator of the venture relative to competing solutions.

The business that receives investment should also have demonstrated the performance of its technology and product, ideally in a relevant customer operating environment, and may have already certified or be planning to certify its product. The business case presented should be profitable in order to offer a decent return to the fund. Attractive entry values and good exit potential are necessary to enable a decent return to the investor.

Impact Parameters

Impact parameters will be key in the identification of the possible deals for consideration. The impact will be in the forms of jobs created, the availability of the product to people who could not otherwise have access to the goods and services, the increase in yield in agriculture, tax revenues generated and so on.

The investor should have in place impact criteria set in advance based on requirements of the investors. There is a more detailed discussion on impact measurements in this chapter. When undertaking investment in Africa, it is critical that the investors consider the environmental and social impacts of the target companies. This is one area that if ignored may lead to significant consequences on the side of the investors. Historically, this has been ignored, especially during the due diligence stage.

Cognizant of this issue, investors are going the extra mile by having a social and environmental criterion that helps to select the potential targets from investments. In addition, they set aside an exclusion list that will define business that they cannot invest in.

Such businesses include those using hazardous materials; for instance agribusinesses that use synthetic chemicals or biopathogens without valid licenses from Pest Control Products Boards (PCPB), business involved in any activity that leads to physical involuntary resettlement of people or loss of assets or access to assets, or loss of livelihoods and sources of income. Others are businesses whose activities result in harmful impact on physical and cultural resources (historical, archaeological and cultural heritage sites, etc.) through excavations, removal of natural forests or reclamation of wetlands or ecologically sensitive habitats.

Other considerations to be taken into account at this point include an honest assessment of the targeted outcomes such as environmental impact; jobs created and the resolution of long-standing social problems in the investee community.

Management Parameters

The quality of management will be the critical factor to consider when assessing an investment. The quality of management could be reviewed from both objective and subjective perspectives. The assessment should be done using both the formal channels as well as the informal channels.

As a general rule the entrepreneur should be passionate and capable about building the enterprise, and open to working with investors to help increase the value of the company. The entrepreneur should have a significant investment (i.e., 'skin in the game') in the business.

The skills of the entrepreneur should be aligned with the needs of the company that s/he is leading. The entrepreneur should be ethical and have a good reputation amongst his/her peers.

When assessing the fitness of the management of the investee, it is also good to broaden the same assessment to the board of firm, in order to make sure that governance policies are aligned to industry best practice. The assessment should have scope to check on the technical skills, commercial skills and interpersonal skills of key management personnel in the firm.

The management of the potential investee company can be assessed in a variety of ways, including meetings and discussions with the management team, referrers and others who know the team and/or business (ideally these people would be well known to the investor) and by reviewing public records. It is important to consider what the entrepreneur/management team has invested in the company themselves.

An investee who is reluctant to put their own funds into their business is usually a red flag and suggests they might be the type of business people who are only playing along in order to access funds from external investors. The portion of shareholding held by the management should be large enough to incentivize them sufficiently to drive the business forward.

It is important to check what other ventures (if any) the entrepreneur/management team is involved in currently and how much time they are spending on these ventures and how such ventures relate to the venture in question. There is a possibility that the entrepreneur could be spread too thin by serial investments in other ventures. This can also result in a situation where the funds received for this particular investment are diverted to other endeavors of the entrepreneur at the expense of the investor.

The vision for the business from the perspective of the entrepreneur and management is also key in shaping the investment. The vision should converge with that of the investor and if there is misalignment, there is need to ensure that it is aligned before the funds are disbursed.

In my experience, it is clear that lack of vision convergence is one of the biggest contributors to failure for impact investing. On this subjective perspective, there is a need to define what makes management team successful. The key elements will include the assessment of the level of passion and energy displayed by the founder and the management teams for the investee companies, and the attitude of the team. Remember that for a winning team, there must be both winning attitude and perseverance.

Case Study of Investment Criteria

Here, we can refer to a case study of KCIC Early Stage Financing Mechanism vehicle (ESFM) that is currently being piloted. In 2017, due to the limited availability of financing for early-stage climate-smart investments in Kenya, the vehicle was seeded with a US$100,000 fund from the Autodesk Foundation with an additional US$200,000 from the Danish Government.

The facility aims to provide financing to scalable climate-smart business that are post-revenue and that have the potential to scale.

In addition to the Autodesk Foundation funding, The Danish Government through the Kenya country program on green growth and employment provided a total of US$12 million to KCIC of with a third of the funds allocated for financing various facilities including the KCV, which is a fund that aims to provide scaling businesses with financing.

The facility is aimed at investing in post-revenue innovative businesses game-changing companies that are working to accelerate the country's progress in achieving its green growth agenda through reducing poverty and improving livelihoods, climate mitigation and adaptation technologies.

Enterprises that meet the following criteria should be identified:

- **Geography**: Be located in or have significant operations or impact in Kenya.
- **Sectors**: Operate in one of our investment sectors of agribusiness, water management and renewable energy.
- **Stage**: Be an early-stage company that is making revenues. We will rarely invest in pure start-up companies with no revenues.
- **Investment size**: Should be seeking investment capital in the range of US$10,000–US$100,000, structured as either debt or equity.
- **Strong management team**: Have a strong and experienced management team with the skills, will, and vision to execute the business plan and unyielding ethics.
- **Environmental/social impact**: Make a product or deliver a service that addresses climate change or a critical need for the poor in our sectors and geographic focus.
- **Financial sustainability potential**: Have a clear business model that demonstrates the potential for financial sustainability within a five to ten-year period, including the ability to cover operating expenses with operating revenues.
- **Scale potential**: Be able to demonstrate a clear path to scale for the number of end users over the period of our investment, and be positioned as one of the leading service providers in the market.

The Investment Approval Process

Potential investments are identified by the Client Services (CSS) team within KCIC's portfolio. All investments go through an initial due diligence process in which the potential investment opportunity is vetted and discussed by the CSS team. For those investments that pass the initial deliberation stage, the client lead produces an investment memo which entails a review of the promoter/enterprise in the general areas of management, financial viability, operations, environmental/social impact, accounting and legal and, finally, the additionality of the funding.

Investment opportunities are then presented to the internal committee acting as the investment committee, which will provide a CIP. The CIP is give the CSS team the authority to carry out further due diligence on the proposed investment case.

Fig. 6.4 Investment appraisal process

Once the further due diligence is completed, there are additional discussions that will normally guide revisions to the funding proposal before submission to the board, which is ultimately responsible for the approval or rejection of investment opportunities.

The process is illustrated in Fig. 6.4.

Financing Instruments

All things considered, investors should seek to achieve an optimal transaction structure. The transactions should be efficient from the three main perspectives of investment returns and distribution of the returns, business control, and the exit. Typically, a variety of investment instruments are used by impact investment funds, ranging from debt, to quasi-equity to equity. In certain cases, a royalty is added in order to enhance returns.

Given that not every entrepreneur is open to ceding, equity investors will need to consider the use of a range of investment instruments that are a hybrid of debt and equity with self-liquidating components (e.g., redeemable/convertible loan notes or redeemable/convertible preference shares) and cash flow-based financing. These should be flexible enough in the payback structure to enable the business to grow—typically, this is something most investors are less flexible on.

They should also not deter potential co-investors and follow-on funders by being too onerous on the company in terms of obligations.

Finally, whichever instrument is chosen should realize returns that are commensurate with the investment risk and consistent with the overall portfolio return strategy.

ESFM provides debt, equity and hybrid funding on a case-by-case basis upon assessment of needs for the opportunities. In **Equity Financing**, ESFM provides equity seed funding for the development and start-up phase for clean technology enterprises.

This is the earliest stage of venture funding, which enables the enterprise to meet its financial obligations while getting started. The primary objective for providing this financing will be to get the enterprise to the point where they are able to raise money on a larger scale, at which stage KCIC will play the role of introducing and facilitating investment by later-stage investors.

The investment strategy would comprise, among others, a number of particulars as shown below. The investment size ranges from US$10,000–US$100,000, for a minority stake of between 5 and 10% in the enterprises funded. Drawdowns are based on agreed milestones.

Investments will be based on negotiated valuation, based on the stage of the enterprise. It will also be structured to facilitate further fundraising by the enterprise on a larger scale.

In **Debt Financing**, ESFM focuses on KCIC's enterprises in all phases of development—that is, start-up, early stage and growth of clean-technology enterprises. ESFM in this case will provide direct financing for working capital and for asset financing up to a maximum of US$100,000.

When providing working capital financing, ESFM provides debt facilities to companies against confirmed invoices/orders/contracts that can be independently verified, and from credible/pre-vetted vendors. The funding is structured in various windows, which include short-term financing periods (maximum of 180 days per financing cycle) and competitive pricing (1–2% interest per month) with ticket sizes of up to a maximum of US$25,000 per client.

For **Asset Financing**, which is a type of lending that provides business assets such as equipment, machinery and vehicles as security for a debt financing, ESFM provides funding to companies to purchase assets that KCIC will hold a charge (as security) until the loan is fully repaid. This is structured as a financing period of 2–3 years, with competitive pricing of up to 10% per annum, and ticket sizes of up to a maximum of US$100,000 per client.

ESFM also offers **Convertible Debt**, which enables it to take advantage of investing in companies with the potential to grow but for which valuation may be an issue at the point of investing. Conversion for this will be triggered based on milestones such as revenue thresholds or fundraising from other investors by the entity.

This line of credit is structured to be subordinated to bank debt, with ticket sizes up to a maximum of US$100,000 per client.

The investee also gets a 2–3 year repayment holiday, with the interest rate coming in at a competitive 3–5% per annum. In addition, ESFM offers 2–3 years' interest holiday (interest to be rolled up).

However, no interest is charged if the debt is converted. If it is not converted, the loan is normally paid back in two equal instalments (in the third and fourth year) including accrued interest.

Another form of financing available to investees is a guarantee facility, meant to support medium-sized businesses and small-scale infrastructure projects (SSIPs). ESFM provides loan guarantee facilities for clean technology enterprises, KCIC acting as a first loss guarantor, and also bringing in other MSME guarantee providers and financing partners, such as banks, to unlock financing to medium-sized businesses and SSIPs. This will typically be for investments above the US$100,000 maximum threshold for ESFM.

For this facility, therefore, ESFM will not be providing direct finance (partly due to the relatively large amounts involved), but will structure facilities that catalyze/unlock financing for such enterprises.

The intent is for ESFM, as a first-loss guarantor and jointly with other guarantors, to participate in the financing risk and provide the financing partners/banks with a highly risk-mitigated financing instrument. On this facility, ESFM provides a 10% first-loss guarantee in favor of a bank or other lender. An external guarantee provider with a focus on clean technology enterprises provides a further credit guarantee to the bank on a pari-passu basis for, say, 50%.

KCIC looks to collaborate with partners such as African Guarantee Fund, SIDA Loan Guarantee facility, African Trade Insurance Agency, USAID's Development Credit Authority Guarantee Facility, Nordic Development Fund Guarantee Facility, and other such schemes on this line of support to businesses.

Based on this risk mitigation and security over the equipment, the bank is able to provide the financing required by the enterprise.

Other Considerations in the Investment Criteria Include

Diversification

As impact investors develop their investment strategies, it is important for them to consider the risk management as a key pillar of their success. One possible way to manage the risk is to have a proper portfolio diversification strategy within the fund or the investment vehicle. The diversification may be in terms of the sectors, countries, deal size and so on.

Depending on the funds available for investment, it will be useful for the investment vehicle to consider the amount of exposure is will to take in form of investment in any single investment. Typically, most of the funds have limited the amount of exposure so that it is not more than 10% of the total funds under management in one investment.

The stage of the investee company is another facet that can be considered from the perspective of risk management; for instance, no more than 25% of the funds should be channeled to early-stage investment. Diversification could also be in the form of a mixed offering of financial instruments, as described above. There is need for the fund manager to consider which instruments to invest in and at what proportions.

Valuations

The determination of the value for the investment is a key component of the investment process. The valuation will help the managers to determine what value to report as well as help in decision making, especially where follow-on investment or co-investment are possibilities.

Various valuation methods exist that often require assumptions and can provide a relatively broad range of values.

Valuation is more of an art than a science and will typically require considerable discussion and negotiation between the parties.

The valuation process and procedure may take a significant management time for the investors and it is advisable to keep the process as simple as possible.

Active Post-Investment Management

When the process of investment evaluation is completed, the next task ahead of the investor is to disburse the funds as well as manage the investment in such a way that it increases the value in terms of impacts expected.

In most of the deals in Africa, this is the start of the hand-holding period as most of the investee companies are still in the nascent early stage where the biggest value to them is sometimes the hand holding for success—this is worth more than the value of the money provided.

Once the deals have been concluded, there is a need to manage the relationship and to add value to the social enterprises. This calls for hand holding especially where the capacity of the entrepreneur is not that great.

In most cases, I have had the indication from the entrepreneurs that they are always looking for more than the money.

The deal making was about money but the post-investment stage is about what value can be added to the business. This support will include governance issues, business advisory issues such as marketing, distribution, human resources management and so on.

It could also call for networking the entrepreneurs with institutions and people who may be relevant. The fact that an outsider is investing in the social enterprises is seen as an endorsement and comes with the benefit of the blue stamp.

To be able to provide the support, there is need for the investors to set up a TA facility, which will help in supporting the businesses.

In most cases, social enterprises are high risk in nature, mainly because they have not firmed up their business models as well as fully testing their services or products. There are also other challenges that this kind of business will undergo, which will require more hand holding.

If an investor is engaged at this stage of the business, there is certainly a need to provide some TA to the business. The TA will help to increase the chances of scaling, and enhance the impacts expected from the business as well as the potential for faster and better returns on investments.

Technical Assistance Facility and Its Benefits in Impact Investing

For one to be successful in impact investing, there must be a provision of TA. If, for instance, one is setting up an impact fund in Africa, there is need to have TA resources that will be utilized to hand-hold the business to success—the absence of such a fund will definitely reduce the level of success of the fund.

In order to be able to maintain the economies of the funds, I will suggest that the TA resources should be separate from the investment resources and hence there should be a TA fund, which could be funded separately from the investment resources.

When setting up a TA fund, there are a number of considerations that need to be considered, mainly the TA needs and benefits, model and funding.

After the investment, there is the baseline support that is normally provided by the investment team sitting on the board of the investee company. In this case, the investor will determine if the investment team is the best placed to play the board role or whether they will have an external party sitting on the board.

The norm is to have the investment team sitting on the board, ensuring that the investment management team have regular contact with the investee company. On the other hand, the TA could comprise a specific service provided by a third party, such as a consultancy on a given area, for the provision of services such as financial management and so on.

This additional support would be covered by the TA facility. This support would be recommended by the investment management team based on the needs of the investee and would be provided by a supplier with sufficient expertise to deliver the prioritized support task(s).

TA funding could be structured in various forms. For instance, it could be recovered in part or in full from the investee over time. TA costs could also treated in variety of other ways as we shall see below.

They could be included in the initial fund investment amount (note there may be push back from companies regarding this option, even though some investors use this approach, e.g., GroFin). These funds can also be provided as an interest-free loan to the investee company, or by a separate grant-funded TA facility, which provides the TA support as a grant to the investee (in which case the investee may commit to invest time but typically not cash to enable this TA support).

Typically, the TA costs would range from 5–30% of the initial investment amount and TA support would typically be delivered within 12–24 months.

When setting up a fund, it is critical to ensure that 10–20% of the overall investment amount would be provided as TA support. TA funding should be governed in such a way that it meets the needs of the investee companies as well as the needs of the fund. The investment management team together with the investee management team would recommend areas for TA support and the amount of support, based on their engagement with the company.

In the pre-investment due diligence process stage and shortly after engaging with the investee companies after the investment, much of the TA needs or expected needs should generally become clear to the fund and TA needs are identified. Once the areas are identified, there is need to present these needs to the committee or governance vehicle that is in charge of the implementation of the TA facility for approval and guidance.

TA can add significant value to the impact fund and investee companies if delivered well, but on the same note, can be a drain on a fund's resources if it is not prudently deployed. The value of TA is likely to go beyond what the company or investment management team will be able to deliver on their own.

Some of the benefits of well-executed TA will include much more prioritized market focus, stronger sales pipeline and strategy, refined business model, protected and prioritized intellectual property rights (IP), stronger team and board, improved financial management, new industrial relationships and de-risked supply chain.

In post-investment management, the investor can also grow the business through mentorship and governance.

In addition, the investor will act as a business advisor with the aim of helping the business to achieve its growth objectives. Normally, the impact fund will assign its investment officers responsibility for managing the relationship between the investment vehicle and specific portfolio companies.

This relationship will include, but will not be limited to coordinating TA provision and mentoring, sitting in the board of the investee companies as well as hand holding the business to grow.

Impact fund managers will therefore need to have a well-established mechanism for supporting the investee companies. This is even more important when the funder is the main investor in a transaction and this calls for active management and sitting on the board of the investee company with the aim of increasing the value as well as the impacts from the transaction.

The support to the business may evolve over time; it is likely to be higher at the inception, and then its evolution may show an appropriate decrease over the life of the investment.

Where there is co-investment, the role is shared among investors. Again, where the deal forms as a result of co-investment between various investors, there is need to consider the merits of active versus passive investment management from the funds perspective.

This will be shaped by the experience of the co-investors, as a result of their prior experience in the investee's particular sector or from the experiences of their respective management teams.

In cases where there is follow-on investment, it is possible that the initial investors will take a more passive role and let the new investors—depending on their capability—run the show in terms of managing the transaction.

This is especially the case when a bigger fund injects follow-on capital into the transaction.

Most of the active management support will be carried out under the umbrella of TA. The investor will be involved in the decision-making process of the firms through board representation, which will call for active participation in strategy development of the investee companies.

The investors will also play a big role in introducing the business to relevant contacts who will help in the execution of the day-to-day business of the investee company.

The impact investor has the role of helping the management of the investee companies to resolve issues and challenges that may be blocking them from growing the business.

The challenges that affects the business will identified and discussed during the annual business planning sessions, board meetings as well as during the regular reviews which is normally done as a joint efforts by the management and, the board of the investee company which will include the representative of the impact fund.

Realisation of Value

Finally, in this chapter, we look at how to realise value from a fund's investment in a particular business. Most of the realization of returns will be through the use of innovative self-liquidating structures that also allow for some additional benefits.

The exit mechanism should be agreed upon where possible in advance to ensure that the expectations of both the investee company and the investors are aimed at avoiding a legal tussle during the exits. In addition, it would be agreed for the fund management to continue to be involved in monitoring over the period of the investment.

The evaluation will consider the value at risk from a particular investment as well as looking at the possible exit opportunities. In most cases, the impact funds will consider the exit mechanisms that will ensure that the same level of higher impacts is created, even after the exit.

Making an exit from an African business can be a tricky affair at the best of times, mainly due to the lack of alternative local investors looking to actively take up ownership of businesses at the post-start-up stage.

Africa has also come to be seen as a frontier space for investors, with the highest return being made by those who identify an opportunity early and

Table 6.1 Exit mechanisms available to an impact investor

Trade sale	Sale to another company, perhaps in the same industry.
Company repurchase	Buy-back of shares by the company or the company management.
Secondary sale	Sale to another investment vehicle.
Self-liquidating mechanisms	Debt investment, where the equity is repurchased progressively with the cash flows generated by the company.
IPO	Listing in a stock exchange and sale of shares to the public.

invest in it. Private equity funds in particular have perfected the art of early entry and exit after fattening the business.

As an impact investor, there is the added factor of having to assess whether the investment has had the desired impact before moving it on to the next investor.

As noted above, the exit mechanism is complicated, since it is not a requirement to pass on an investment to another responsible impact investor who will not roll back the gains that your investment has had on the environment and society. That said, there are a number of exit mechanisms available to an impact investor, as we see in the Table 6.1.

The Initial public offerings (IPO) is not a typical exit mechanism for an impact investor, but theoretically it remains a possibility. There are not many cases that have reached the IPO stage and the African markets are not that developed to accommodate IPOs, especially for the small- and medium-sized businesses—a classification to which many impact investments belong.

Looking back, the most popular mode of exit is self-liquidating financing, followed by the secondary sales, meaning sale to a bigger fund.

Conclusion

The design stage of a fund is the most critical in determining the success or failure of a venture. As discussed, the alignment of strategy and core competencies is crucial for anyone designing a fund. It will certainly save headaches down the road. We have seen a good number of funds treading water when they realise they took on more than they were equipped to handle.

It is important to understand the market and the size of the opportunity on offer, since this will inform growth assumptions and business valuation, saving money in the start-up stage and helping to align investment amounts with the expected returns.

We have also dealt with the importance of deal origination, which informs all the other aspects of forming a fund. This will involve identifying deals and determining the type of fund that will be most suitable to deploy.

Often, I have seen investors who have, in a sense, 'overinvested' in the initial stages, only to find out later that due to this the period it takes to make a full return on investment is too long, and that, in chasing the break-even, they have little resources to put into the impact-related activities of the business.

It is also important to stress that accessing accurate financial reports of a company prior to investing in it is critical before the fund is designed and deployed, especially in a market like Africa, which can sometime throw unpleasant surprises your way.

As mentioned, owner participation in an investment is also an important barometer for an impact investor. A serious entrepreneur should have a significant equity stake. Another thing we shall keep insisting on, and which will also be discussed in Chapter 8, is that the fund should be designed an eye on the exit mechanisms that will be available.

It is important to be flexible, as highlighted in Chapter 2, in order to accommodate the unique elements of the impact investing space. Once the fund is established, it is necessary to carry out a few housekeeping tasks that will ensure its continued success.

A board of advisers or a board of directors will be needed to oversee important facets such as corporate governance. An IC is also necessary, tasked with ensuring that the objectives of both the investors and the investee are met. The fund management team, while ensuring that the fund is properly run, is the team that will ensure that the desired impact is being felt as a result of the investment.

Once all of this is in place, all that remains is running the fund on a day-to-day basis and, as we shall see in Chapter 7, keeping an eye on whether the fund and the investment is having the desired impact.

7

Measuring Impact for Continued Growth

As we have seen in the preceding chapters, impact investing is taking the center stage with helping to push forward the development agenda in Africa. More and more leaders in finance, philanthropy, business and government are looking for ways to help solve society's problems through impacts resulting from their investments.

In order to attract and pool more private money, there is need to have a well-established mechanism for measuring impact as a way of providing evidence that it is making the intended difference. Effective impact measurement generates value for all impact investment stakeholders, mobilizes greater capital, and increases the transparency and accountability for the impact delivered.

Why Measure Impact?

Investors in Africa need to be able to build the case that impact investing is changing livelihoods. By providing a transparent measure of the transformation that an investment is having on ordinary lives, one can easily make a case for further financing, which is especially true for open-ended funds that rely on additional investment to remain viable in the long term. Failure to do this will mean that the business case for impact investing will not be in place and hence the case for further financing will not be justified.

Traditionally, internal rate of return (IRR) was the benchmark for measuring the performance of an investment. With the emergence of the impact

© The Author(s) 2018
E. Mungai, *Impact Investing in Africa*,
https://doi.org/10.1007/978-3-030-00428-6_7

investing asset class, however, this mode of measurement is proving quite inadequate.

There is now an additional requirement to broaden the measurement of the returns to include both the social and the environmental returns.

Investors are keen to know the contribution of their investment and, in the past, some of the investors have requested photos and stories of the happy customers that the investments are creating.

This type of information has formed the basis for good dinner table stories and, as a result, more and more people have been pushed towards investing in the sector through soft persuasion, away from the usual formal boardroom presentations that can often fail to capture the real essence of an impact investment.

The growth of impact investing will depend on how well the investors are able to illuminate their success and the transformation that such investments are producing.

The stories emanating from the investment cases will be key and this will be in the form of the data on sustainable development, as well as reflections on the case studies. It is therefore critical for there to be a proper definition of impact and for it to be reported in a more consistent way. However, this is one of the major challenges facing the sector.

Fortunately, there are various standard measures that can be employed to fill the gap, even though the sector is not yet sufficiently developed for there to be one standout approach.

In most simple impact investment cases, entrepreneurs and investors are able to measure and report impact in a consistent manner. The drawback of this is the fact that both are limited in comparing the performance of the investments in terms of the impacts that are realized, especially in greenfield areas for the investor.

Performance measures need to be simplified and need to address the needs of the impact investors. Impact will vary from business to business and should be therefore be handled on a case-by-case basis.

For investors looking to measure environmental and social impacts of the investments, there is a popular framework provided by GIIN and IRIS, as well as others developed specifically by a given investor. This does not negate the need for a standardized impact measuring framework that will enable investors to compare the effectiveness and efficiency of the impact investments and fund managers.

However, having a standardized mechanism of impact measurement is a complex matter considering that the impact investee companies range in terms of the size and scope of their activities and hence standardizing might not make a lot of sense for some of them.

Similarly, the impact investee companies target different levels of impact return, as opposed to a situation where those targeting a financial return only focus on one parameter—the IRR—which has a standard formula of measurement. The net effect of this complexity is the development of proprietary impact measurement frameworks, which are normally expensive to develop and do not make economic sense for the small-scale impact investors.

The lack of internal data management systems within the enterprises is also a challenge in impact measurement. The impact is normally reported by the investee companies, which in most cases are SMEs that have no capability of developing impact measurement and reporting frameworks. This is a challenge to the integrity of the data provided, if at all any is provided in the first place.

Verification of the impact reported by the investors, especially from third parties, will therefore go a long way to adding credibility to the data provided. Unfortunately, not many funds have been involved in data verification which is much needed especially in the cases where proprietary models for reporting have been implemented.

Data verification is an expensive affair, and thus very few verifiers are providing the services in Africa. Benchmarking of the results is also another challenge on the African continent.

This is due to the fact that the data on impact is not readily available and hence a benchmark cannot be developed easily. There is also the reality that some fields of investment, such as technology, are relative newcomers, lacking a backstory that can be used as a measure of impact.

The data on impact belongs to the fund managers and the investors and, in many cases, is not made public and hence the development of benchmarks is a real challenge.

Benchmarks, while hard to develop, will nonetheless be useful in measuring the effectiveness and efficiency of various funds. Measuring impact is not a linear process, but rather will require more iterative processes for both investors and investees to be able to arrive at the most optimal way of reporting and measuring the impact. This will require the purpose of the impact measurement to be well articulated.

In most cases, there is no clarity on the purpose for measuring impact, especially for the recipients of funding for whom administrative costs are seen as a drain on returns. Many are often blind to the fact that measuring impact to show success attracts more funds, and the fact that investee companies can use the impacts to showcase their social and environmental business model and their contributions to livelihoods.

Framework for Measuring Impact Investments Today

Impact will normally take the form of higher tax revenues, more jobs created, mitigation of carbon emissions and so on. This will require the investors as well as the investee companies to keep track of all these elements without losing focus on running a profitable enterprise.

In other words, impact investing clearly requires a commitment to the provision of positive social or environmental targets. Therefore, in order to be able to measure the impact, it is necessary to have a proper definition, measurement and reporting system, which will be implemented in the form of a monitoring and evaluation (M&E) strategy.

A M&E strategy will provide the process and outputs for impact measurement. The strategy will consist of various frameworks that are based on a Theory of Change (ToC).

The frameworks will include the Logical Framework (LF), Results Framework (RF) and Performance Framework (PF) of the fund or investment vehicle. The strategy will also outline the baseline data, current and future analysis of data, knowledge and information management and roles and responsibilities of the investor and investee companies in determining and measuring the impact of an investment.

The strategy should not only be designed for the purposes of tracking and measuring progress but also as an investor management tool. The strategy will require a review after every two years to ensure that it remains relevant to the needs of investor, their partners and the investee companies.

The impact measurement strategy is normally aimed at strengthening the impact investor's capacities in evidence-based programming, M&E of the resulting impacts. It will also ensure that evidence-based M&E is understood as part of the management cycle and as the best way of measuring progress, detecting problems, correcting them, improving performance, accountability and learning.

The strategy will also help in monitoring and providing feedback on the implementation progress, while the evaluation processes will provide feedback to investors and other stakeholders on the results and lessons learned.

The knowledge that will be generated by the investor on effective investing approaches and lessons learned will be captured and disseminated internally and externally to collaborating institutions, investee companies and the general public.

The impact measurement frameworks should be anchored on a ToC. This is a logical model that will present the impact investor resources, activities, and the short and long-term outcomes. This is a useful tool, and can help to clarify goals and communicate the basics of how the impact investor expects his or her interventions to translate to real social benefit.

Developing a good ToC means coming up with a clear and testable hypothesis about how change will occur that not only allows the investor to be accountable for results, but also gives an assurance that the results have higher credibility as they were predicted to occur in a certain way. It is also a visual representation of the change the investor wants to see in the investee companies and a roadmap of how they expect the change to come about.

This ToC is therefore a blueprint for evaluation, with measurable indicators of success identified, carrying an agreement among stakeholders about what defines success and what it takes to get there. From my experience working in impact investment circles around Africa, I have seen that having a good ToC is a powerful communication tool to capture the complexity of the impact investor initiative, which is important in explaining the need to push capital into these investments to skeptical investors at a time when they could be opting for more traditional investment options.

As a framework, it can be used to check milestones and stay on course, while documenting the lessons learned about what really happens in an impact investment project for posterity. It can also be used to keep the process of implementation and evaluation transparent, so that everyone knows what is happening and why it is going the way it is. Therefore, when preparing reports for funders, policymakers and other stakeholders, a ToC is essential.

Principles to Consider Before Developing Measurement Strategy

As impact investors develop the impact measurement strategy, it is important that the strategy should have the following key principles:

Ensure evidence-based conclusions: Conclusions drawn from impact measurement processes should be based on consistent data gathering, analysis,
information, or knowledge that responds to the measurement requirements.

Develop a balanced emphasis on learning processes and accountability: Impact
measurement activities should be focused on results in order to improve
impact whilst also building learning processes as well as ensuring accountability to all relevant stakeholders.

Come up with a participatory approach: A participatory approach will promote investor and investee ownership, commitment and strong capacities.
The measurement process should respect the voice and perspectives of all
key stakeholders (both internal and external).

Make use of practical and cost-effective processes: Impact investors should maximize the use of in-house skills and resources as and when necessary.

Provide a measure of change that is understandable and clear: The impact
measurement strategy should enable investors and other stakeholders
to understand what change was achieved (also to what extent and how
change occurred) as a result of their investment and other interventions.

Capture negative change as a part of lessons learned: The strategy will allow
for the tracking of negative change, reversals, backlash and unexpected
events that can derail the objectives of investor. These will be captured
early enough and mitigate the actions taken.

Case Study: Kenya Climate Innovation Centre

As an illustration of the ToC, we can look at a case derived from the KCIC.
This is not a typical impact investment scenario but it will provide a good
example of how to develop a ToC.

In 2015, KCIC embarked on a fundraising mission from donors—mainly
development partners, foundations and family offices in Europe and the
USA. To be able to put forward the case for funding, it was necessary for
KCIC to develop a ToC that formed the basis of the impact measurement,
the details of which we can see in the Fig. 7.1.

The inputs that are not depicted in the diagram are the activities that the
KCIC conducts on a daily basis, which deliver the outputs shown at the bottom of the figure. These outputs relate to the activities that are seen to contribute to the success of businesses, especially those that are in the clean tech
sector.

For example, access to finance is a major challenge for businesses. There
will be many activities to be undertaken at the input level, such as proof of

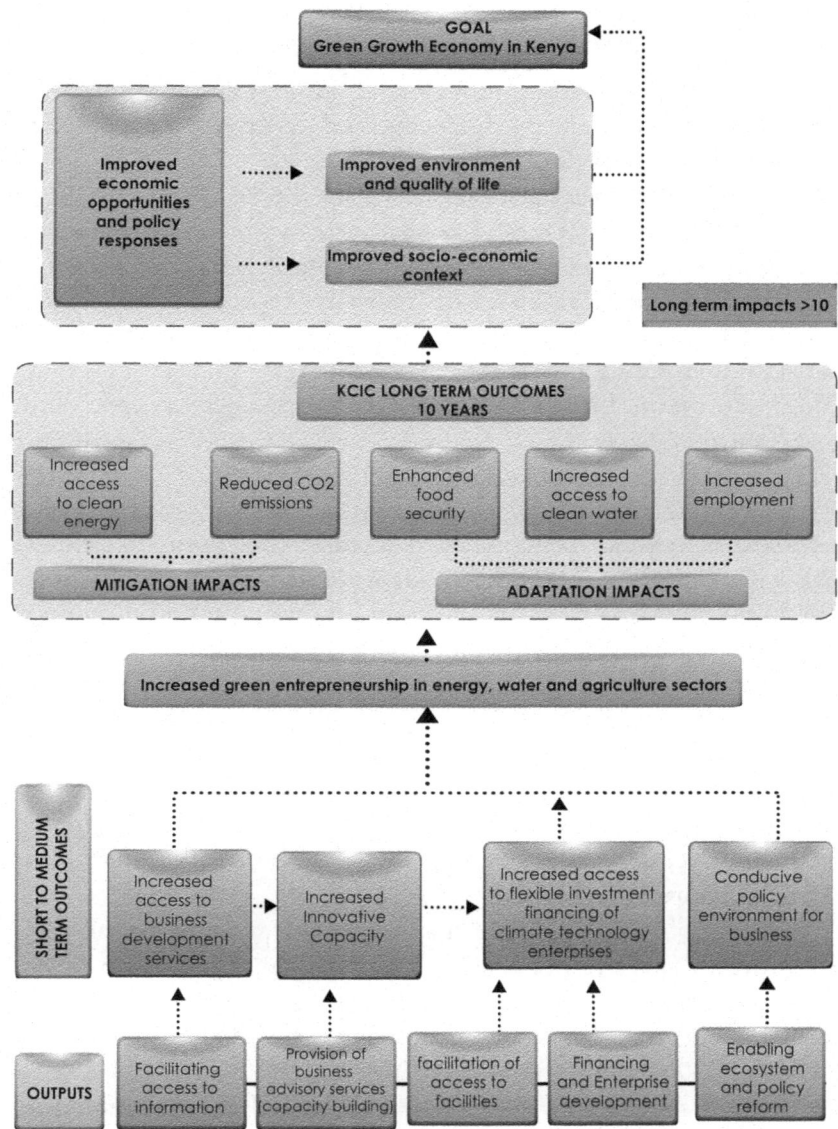

Fig. 7.1   Kenya Climate Innovation Centre ToC

concept financing, syndications and financial modelling that will result in the business being able to raise financing. In this case, business being able to raise financing will be considered as an output under the output level, which is the representation at the bottom of the chart. In addition, job creation is at a much higher level (outcome) as opposed to it being an output as this happens when businesses are able to raise financing.

The outputs level is in line with the services that are provided by KCIC, which are aimed at facilitating SMEs in the clean tech sector, namely facilitating access to information, provision of business advisory services, facilitation of access to facilities, financing and enterprise development and enabling ecosystem and policy reform.

The outputs are interrelated as shown by the arrows connecting them with the short-term outcomes. The next level of the ToC is the outcomes, which were divided into four short-term changes: increased access to business development services, increased innovative capacity, increased access to investment financing of climate technology enterprises and a conducive policy environment for business.

These short-term changes are then expected to increase green entrepreneurship in the energy, water and agriculture sectors in the medium term, which is typically about five years.

This means that there will be a greater number of small and medium enterprises willing and being enabled to offer climate-smart technologies, which will result in mitigation and adaptation benefits in the long term—i.e. in 10 years' time.

Mitigation impacts relate to reductions in carbon emissions and increased access to clean energy. Adaptation impacts are usually found within the socio-economic sectors where changes in livelihoods are observed as a result of increased adaptive capacity.

Hence, enhanced food security, increased access to clean water and increased employment and household incomes will enhance households' adaptive capacity as a result of being able to access climate-smart technologies being incubated by KCIC.

In the longer term (i.e. more than 10 years), we expect that there will be improved economic opportunities and policy responses to businesses, improved environment and quality of life and an improved socio-economic context leading to a green growth economy, which is Kenya's vision as per the Vision 2030 medium-term plan (2018–2022).

As we can see, based on the example above and the explanations earlier in the chapter, the ToC has become more popular in the impact investing sector with more and more investors looking at the ToC as the basis for evaluation and measuring of impacts.

A case in point is the Acumen Fund, which uses a logic model—in this case the ToC–to look into the assumptions made by the investee companies in delivering impacts. It is also used for the purposes of assessing risks, the factors that could curtail the achievements of impacts from the interventions the fund through investments.

For each investment, the Acumen team outlines what they think the biggest impact risks are and then comes up with strategies to help monitor the achievement of the target impacts and manage any risks that may arise. Under the ToC, Acumen will establish the specific measures and actions for input, activities, output, outcomes and impacts.

We can now look at the different frameworks that can be employed in measuring impact.

Logical Framework

Once the ToC is in place, there is need to develop a LF, like the one being employed by Acumen. The LF for the impact measurement summarizes the key features of impact investing strategy and is best used by investors and the investee companies in the planning and decision-making processes.

It is meant to be a dynamic tool that shows at a glance, the main outputs and outcomes, the indicators that will measure the progress, and also where the information will be collected from, or sources of evidence. It also highlights important assumptions that have been made for the impact investing strategy to realize its overall objective.

The intention of the LF is to capture the intermediate and long-term outcomes from the ToC so that a logical flow can be established with the indicators and with the changes expected. In addition, LF attempts to capture the complex nature of impact investment impact measurement so that comprehensive information is captured, documented and disseminated through a lesson-learning process.

The indicators in the LF will need to be reviewed, especially in a midterm review. This is to ensure that they are still relevant and that progress towards outcomes will be possible with specific indicators.

Results Framework

The RF has been designed as a tracking tool for day-to-day management. The format is similar to the LF but with yearly targets included. In addition, it will contain indicator definitions (so that any stakeholder will be able to interpret the meaning of the impact numbers). It will also provide the frequency of data collection, assumptions and data collection roles and responsibilities.

A review of the targets set in the RF will need to be carried out annually so that adjustments can be made accordingly. Furthermore, the data collection methods will also need to be reviewed periodically, especially after annual reviews.

Data Collection and Analysis

Finally, when measuring impact, data collection and management is paramount. In maximizing the efficiency of staff and resources, it helps to ensure that there is collection of accurate and reliable data, with focus on the careful management of such data once it has been collected.

The collection, management and analysis of data is often a neglected aspect of impact investing. Rarely will fund managers be found dedicating the time to programme planning and implementation, but this has significant effects on programme effectiveness.

Thus, a system of data collection for each indicator in the log frame needs to be designed and will consist of the person or team responsible for impact measurement filing all the data collection tools centrally for easy access by others.

The data collection tools consist of checklists generated from the monitoring information identified while developing the impact measurement strategy. They need to be tailor-made for each investee company.

The next step is to consolidate all the impact data collected from investee companies systematically against specific indicators. The consolidated data at output and outcome levels will form the basis of expectation for future investments, and will also be used for the analysis to assess how well the investee companies are delivering the expected impacts.

Uses of the Information Collected

The investor or the interested party needs to define use of the data as well as at what stage of investment cycle he or she is at on the investment value chain. This helps when the fund is developing its strategy for the investment fund or investment vehicle—in this case the ToC could be the best way to go about developing the way the impact will flow from the daily operations of the fund.

The data will also be useful for estimating the impact expected from an investment case at the due diligence stage. Measuring the data will also be useful in improving the operations of the funds, especially borrowing from the past lesson on the way the fund delivers impacts.

Managers will also use the data to look into the effectiveness and efficiency of the investments.

In Conclusion

The measurement of impact, therefore, is key in attracting further funding into the impact investment space. It is only by measuring how much transformation a venture has been able to bring to the host community that an investor can convince funders to put in more resources into the line of business.

As previously noted, a lack of a quantifiable impact will mean that the business case for further financing will not be justified. However, we have highlighted a major challenge in achieving this—the lack of a properly defined and consistent mechanism to measure impact.

This issue needs to be addressed by the players in the impact investing ecosystem as a matter of urgency, since the sector is no longer at the stage of taking baby steps, but rather is at the stage where it needs to scale up significantly and move to the next level of growth.

While there are various standard measures that can be employed to fill the gap, the sector is yet to set up one standout approach that can be deployed across various industries, countries or fund types. The question we will have to answer in the next few years is with regard to developing this standard approach.

In a nutshell, we have proposed a number of principles that need to be considered when making a good impact measurement framework. By using evidence-based mechanism to measure impact, it is possible to quantify that the data you have is commensurate with the requirements of the investor. For this, it is necessary to have consistency in your data collection and analysis.

It is also important, as we have noted, that lessons are learnt and applied in the course of an investment. By ensuring that all the lessons learnt are put in practice, you will improve on the accountability to all stakeholders by assuring them that you are following best practice. These will be both the positive and negative lessons.

The measures employed to gauge impact must also be all inclusive, incorporating and respecting the points of view of all the stakeholders.

It is also important to remember to make full use of in-house skills and resources when measuring impact. Apart from the fact that they have ownership of the enterprise, and know the ins and outs better than anyone else, it will also save on resources that would have otherwise been deployed outside in order to get the expertise. Overall, the importance of a good impact measurement mechanism cannot be overstated.

It is this appraisal that will ensure that you keep to the goals of creating impact through your investment.

8

De-risking Your Investments

Investment is a science, but impact investing is an art.

In this section, we shall look at how applying the principles of a good impact investment feeds into lowering the risk involved with making investments in what can be a challenging and tricky environment in Africa. The key thing for impact investors is to be business partners as opposed to financing partners and, in the process, keep a closer and more involved eye on their investment to ensure that it is marrying the need to bring returns with the need to make an impact in society.

Traditional fund managers, investment bankers and private equity managers are not used to this kind of hand-holding and their approach is to wait for the financials and other reports as well as sitting in board meeting in Paris, London, Amsterdam, San Francisco, New York and so on. In impact investment, each case is unique and there is nothing like the one-size-fits-all model as prescribed by the traditional investments. This is usually the most important factor to impact investors should consider when taking stock of the risks they face.

The management of each deal is therefore normally on a case-by-case basis and will require flexibility in terms of how the investor deals with the business and the entrepreneur. It ends up being a relationship and a journey that both the impact investor and the entrepreneur embark on and in which they discover the beauties and the challenges that impact businesses faces. However, it is a relationship in which the investor will need to take the lead, and as we shall see in a case study later in the chapter, be alert to problems arising in the investment and be brave enough to take tough action early to prevent irreversible losses.

© The Author(s) 2018
E. Mungai, *Impact Investing in Africa*,
https://doi.org/10.1007/978-3-030-00428-6_8

It is therefore necessary for the investor be as clear as possible with themselves and with the investee with regard to the expectations and plans for the business. For instance, there are those investors looking for business that will scale in the shortest time possible whilst other are looking at businesses that will be stable and that will grow at the rates of, say, 15% year-on-year.

Take an example of Novastar Ventures, who describe themselves as a catalyst firm assisting the next generation of exceptional entrepreneurs who are designing and executing innovative business models to profitably serve East Africa's aspiring mass market. In a typical investment, they will undertake to invest US$200,000 in businesses that will be able to scale upwards, and which requires up to US$7 million within the first five years and targeting to impact over one million livelihoods.

The investment process does not need to be prescriptive, as is the case for more traditional investments. They recognize that there is a need to learn on the job and allow for the minimum viable project to take course. Technical assistance (TA) is critical and there is where it becomes a journey. It is not normally about the money but rather about taking the journey and hand-holding the business.

The term sheet is sometimes forgotten, and the focus is always to grow the business. This kind of thinking is required for the impact investing and the flexibility that comes with it.

Investors are normally looking for PowerPoint and good Excel sheets when laying the groundwork for an investment, looking to use the numbers and projections in order to gauge risk and look at the opportunity on offer. This will not come from African impact businesses, however.

For instance, remember the fund I spoke about in chapter five, which looked at 240 enterprises in 2016, and only invested in two of them, due to the rigorous outlook of the investment team, which unfortunately was made up of bankers who were looking for perfect Excel progression, good audited financial statements and proper business strategies. With a better understanding of their environment and appreciation of the nature of risks they faced, they would perhaps have made more investments. In the course of applying the wrong medicine to a problem, they may have lost out on discovering the next great African enterprise.

Impact investing, like we said earlier, is about looking at entrepreneurs and having the conviction that they can do the job; it is looking at the products and the potential market. These former investment bankers who turned impact investment managers will, for instance, not be successful unless they transform to be business partners and not worry too much for instance on the terms laid out on terms sheet.

Impact investing is therefore aimed at creating impact but at the same time is aimed at producing some level of commercial returns. The commercial returns are geared towards the sustainability of the investment. It also helps in providing some discipline to the company being invested in. In the past, the continent had been faced with the donation hangover, which has resulted in a lack of financial discipline for companies as they expect more donations than the financial investment.

When impact funds have some level of return expectation, this creates the impression that they are investors and not donors, which is a totally different ball game in terms of the commercial discipline in the investment. It should therefore be the objective of impact investors to aim to realize a return on 'capital' invested through patient, risk-tolerant, tailored financing accompanied by high-touch monitoring and bespoke TA and coaching.

The additions to the provision of financing is what makes impact investing unique compared with other assets classes. Some of the unique characteristics of the impact investor should include the following.

Patience: Consider an investment of up to US$250,000 of funding solution that will enable a target enterprise to propel revenue growth to an 'inflection point'—attracting other bigger investors such as private equity funds and other next stage 'investor'. It will to necessary for investors to cater for 'vibration' and 'cash constraints' on the path to sustainability and revenue stability. This will mean that investors will need to provide for future rounds of financing.

Most of the impact cases will require more financing than was initially estimated, and in this case the investor needs to continue funding the business through future rounds. Investments like M-PESA and D-light have attracted more than five rounds of financing and still are not yet fully scaled.

The impact funds have the option to participate in the future rounds of finance or not. In most cases. more and more funds are participating in the future rounds in order to safeguard their stakes from dilution but, more importantly, to continue being financing and supporting agents of the social enterprises in question.

Risk tolerance: The investor needs to have a higher appetite for risk, which is greater than the risk that the traditional investors will be willing to absorb. This is due to the high-risk nature of start-up and early-stage enterprises. As such, there is also need for the impact investors to have ways of de-risking their investments.

Possible ways of de-risking investments that are also discussed in more detail later in this chapter include selection of the entrepreneur, regular monitoring, hand-holding and mentoring and coaching of the entrepreneur.

It is also important to allow for a 'dry powder' close of 25% of capital invested. Normally, the projections provided by investee companies are very pessimistic and, in most cases, the projections will need to be adjusted upwards. This will call for the financers to provide additional funding in order to be able to implement the actions and activities that had been committed for implementation with the amount investment in the business. This is a commitment rarely made by traditional profit-led investors. This is where the issue of the dry powder will be very useful. When impact investors make a commitment to invest in social enterprises, it is safe to make a provision of 25% of the committed funds for possible cost of overruns or delays in implementation of the project.

Offer tailored finance: Impact funds should offer financing instruments suitable for early-stage businesses, based on a financial model that accounts for what will often be a lower-growth trajectory compared with non-impact investments that do not have to worry about giving back to society.

The focus should also be on self-liquidating mechanisms, which also provides benefits in the life of the business. There is need therefore to tie the expected returns to the success of the business in the form of growth in revenues and cash flows as well as the success in raising more financing.

Offer technical assistance: Post-investment management of deals is a critical success factor for those who want to involve themselves in the impact space. This will be provided in the form of TA and needs to be well structured and planned.

The TA should be targeted and tailored and should add value to the investment. In most cases, TA is provided by a different team from the investment team to maintain some independence. In most structures in sub-Saharan Africa, TA is structured as an interest-free loan to the business.

There is need for proper alignment between the investee and the investor to ensure that the TA is used in the best way possible since there have been instances where the social entrepreneurs have shied away from TA due to the fact that it is repayable, and they feel that there is no need for the proposed TA intervention.

Consider setting a budget of 20% of capital investment for TA. Funding for TA should, where possible, be on a returnable basis (zero coupon loan with reimbursements aligned with financial plan and cash flow). The TA will be used to provide high-touch post-investment support and will be key to investment de-risking on the part of the investor and will be useful for preparing the business to scale. With this in mind, we can now look in more detail at de-risking investments, a key factor in the success of an impact investment.

Investment De-risking

Investors in social enterprises are faced with more risk than is associated with traditional investments. This calls for more careful evaluation and management of the transactions and innovation in dealing with the risk exposures.

Every fund or impact investor should therefore have a guideline on how to manage the risks inherent in their chosen line of investment. The easiest way to manage the risk is to have an inbuilt de-risking mechanism within the investment process. Some of the de-risking mechanisms are discussed below, and we shall also look at an example of an investment made in Uganda by a Danish firm that did not do a proper risk evaluation on the ground before committing funds.

Selection of Entrepreneur and Market Research

Prudent selection of the investment and the investee is the first and most important component of the de-risking process. This is the stage where the investor will ensure that there is a laid-out criterion guiding the transactions that they involve themselves in.

This will require proper analysis of the various ingredients of the deal, including the entrepreneur, the business models, the market to be served by the business, the country of operations and so on.

The entrepreneur is the key component of any transaction and the investor should invest substantial effort in understanding the entrepreneur. The investee should be considered from the perspective of their vision, skills and motivation of establishing the social enterprises. It is necessary to have good chemistry between the investor and the entrepreneur to ensure that the business is properly managed. Some funds have gone to the extent of carrying out a personality test for the entrepreneur that they are backing, and this is used as part of the evaluation.

An example of such funds is the Business Partners International (BPI), which invests a lot of effort into understanding the entrepreneur. This has resulted in a significant reduction of the risk of failure due to entrepreneur selection. It is necessary for the investor to consider these factors vis-à-vis the deal and to evaluate how the various components of the selection contribute to the risk level of the deal.

In most cases, the investors will have access to proper guidelines from previous investments in the same field by other impact investors or data compiled by either government or non-government agencies. These could be in form of the characteristics of the investor, the size of the market, the demand for the product and services and the level of attractiveness of such a market, which will help in determining which deals to invest in and which to avoid.

In the case of Bright Chicks Uganda, we can see how a good and opportune business can be brought to its knees by a lack of appreciation of risk. The project started operations in 2017 with funding from impact investors from Denmark, and in November of the same year had hatched their first batch of chicks.

The core business of Bright Chicks Uganda was to rear chickens for the supply of meat and eggs in the Uganda market. It came into the market with a well thought-out business plan, given that in 2007 there were not many farms in Uganda that were stocking more than 50,000 birds. Therefore, at the time of its establishment, it was the biggest chicken farm in the country, employing over 100 workers. The business started as a rearing farm, which then evolved to incorporate feed processing and a chicken slaughtering facility, which was halal certified.

The business case for the farm was very promising considering that it was looking at the whole value chain of chicken rearing and that there were not many players in the market. At the same time, the competition was very low whilst the demand for the product was more than the project promoters and financers had expected. This demand spanned into the whole of Uganda as well as South Sudan and Congo.

The management of the project ticked all the evaluation boxes including the fact that the promoters were renowned poultry farmers in Denmark with over 20 years' experience in large-scale farming, the location of the farm was less than 50 kilometres from the Ugandan capital Kampala and the raw materials for the feeds production were readily available.

The management and the investors did not foresee many problems and challenges with the project—that is, until the project was underway. The challenges that surfaced early included problems with chicken diseases, poor quality feeds, the low quality of day-old chicks and skill gaps in Uganda. The team realized that the animal husbandry for the Uganda chicken industry was not up to the standards they and expected.

The hit from the quality of day old chicks was two-fold, arising from poor breeding stock and infestation of diseases. The major disease that infected the day-old chick was mycoplasma, which has severe impacts on the birds, especially on growth rate and weight gain, which led to major losses for the company. The net result of all these challenges was high operational costs and high mortality rate for the chickens, which led to operational losses in the early days.

There were also infrastructure challenges, where power supply was unreliable and hence the company had to invest in the generators, which were costly to operate and maintain. Even with their years of experience in poultry farming in Denmark, the lead promoter to the project had never experienced some of the challenges faced in Uganda, which meant that there was a lag time between the identification and solving of the problems.

If there had been a good pool of skilled project managers in Uganda, this could have been resolved quickly, but due to the skill shortage it took time to get through the challenges experienced by the Danes.

Mycoplasma is a disease that was eradicated in Europe many years ago, and the breeder's Danish farms had eradicated this disease many decades prior to coming to Uganda. As a solution, the farm started importing day-old chicks from Kenya, which in itself was a challenge in the sense that it required approval of the ministries in both Kenya and Uganda which took a lot of time to execute and hence further delays in getting the day old chicks.

The feed quality was also very poor due to bad raw material and the producers cheating farmers. This resulted in heavy costs as it took more time for the chicken to reach maturity and add the required weight as a result. It was only at beginning of 2009, after the investors injected more investment capital in a feed production facility, that this problem was resolved.

Investment Performance Reporting

At the investment stage, it is important for the investor and the investee to agree on specific milestones with regard to the transactions and what is expected if the business. This will be in the form of specific parameters that must be achieved by the businesses.

These will include things likes the sales level, inventory levels, customer satisfaction levels; financing and financing structure parameters and so on. Closely monitoring the performance parameters through regular performance reporting will be critical in de-risking the investment.

The investors will be in touch with the reality of the business from the reports provided by management and will be able to get early warning signs when things are not going in the right direction. The investor will want to have quality assurance, which can be achieved by ensuring the correctness of the information provided by the management of the social enterprises.

It is also necessary for the investor to have an appreciation of the time and effort required for the reporting—the level and frequency of reporting—to ensure that that social enterprises are not spending valuable time reporting as opposed to running the business. Most impact investors request quarterly financial and operational reports from the investee companies, and this has been used as way of mitigating the risk on the success of the business as well as giving the investors an opportunity to understand the progress of the business.

Founder's Personal Guarantees

In most cases, the investee businesses do not have the security to provide to the investors. Traditionally, security in the form of collateral has been the common method of de-risking investment, especially favored by lending institutions that otherwise do not have the time or capacity to police the entrepreneur on a full-time basis.

For most social enterprises, security is not existent and hence the investors will have to look for an alternative replacement.

One such effective method is to use personal guarantees from the founders of the business. When one acquires personal guarantees, it means that the founders in their personal capacity will be surcharged in case of default and hence will act as the security to the investment. Although there is not much value on this personal guarantee, psychologically it acts as good measure to align the interests of the founders to those of the investors and ensure that the interests of the investors are aligned to those of the founders and hence the investment is relatively safeguarded.

Investors should also keep an eye on how much they have invested in the business themselves. If they have something to lose in case the business fails, it is safe to assume that they will fight hard to make the business a success. Those investees who have put in very little into their own business could just be out to take investor funds and ride off into the distance.

Contract Terms

Contract terms will also form part of the de-risking mechanism of impact investing. The structuring of the terms of the investment contained either in the shareholder agreement or the loan agreement of the financing provided to a social enterprise will form a way of mitigating the risks. This will be in the form of clauses used for the investment transaction, including the instruments chosen for investment. For instance, where the investment is in the form of a debt instrument, there is a higher chance that the founders will not default. On the other hand, if the investment is an equity investment, there is a chance that the terms of the investee are not so strict that it would result in defaulting.

The terms on the contract could also include representation on the board of the company, which will mean that the investor will be part of the decision making at the company level. However, although the investor may consider putting standard terms of contacts in place for investments, at the same it helps to have the flexibility required to adopt the terms to the specific cases.

Investors should also always seek legal advice on the agreement in the different countries before the agreement are signed. Most of the countries in Africa have different requirements for legal contracts, and the enforceability of the clauses differs from country to country. As such, there is a need to have the legal advice for each jurisdiction to ensure the enforceability of the terms of the investment agreements.

High-Touch Monitoring

Proper monitoring of the investment will act as a way of mitigating the risks that are inherent in the investments. Monitoring should be 'hands on,' meaning that it will more deliberate and with the aim of increasing the value of the social enterprise.

In the PE model, monitoring is normally done at the board level and through reporting. In this case, the investor will be represented in the board of the investee company and will expect standard reports on a monthly, quarterly, semiannual and annual basis.

The story is very different for the impact investing, the investor will need to hand-hold the investee company as they are still at the early stages of their development. This hand-holding will be through the provision of TA—both services and advisory—provided to the company to make it better. In the absence of this, the risk is that the investment will not succeed and hence this forms a major part of the de-risking of the investment.

Impact investors also must avoid the stereotyping common with the PE funds that investee companies only require financing. For impact investments, finances are secondary; what is important is the hand-holding to help the investee companies overcome their challenges and hence increase their chances of success.

Enterprise Budgets

Investee companies will normally provide their work plans and budgets for the year to the investors in advance of the start of the financial year. This will provide the basis of the activities of the business over the next 12 months.

Impact investors need to familiarize themselves with the enterprise's budget and raise questions where the budgets do not make sense. This is normally a good de-risking factor in cases where the investor has a good grasp of the business through the TA. This will mean that the investors understand the business and adds value in the review of the work plans and budgets with the aim of enhancing the value as well as the impacts that can be created by the business.

At the inception of the investment, it is important that the impact investor is provided with an estimation for the financing requirement of the business, as well as how the funds from the investor will be utilized. Closer monitoring of the budgets and works plans will be critical in order to ensure proper management of the business.

There is also a need for the company to have the proper governance structures to approve the budgets and works pans as well as revision and review of the same. With the budgets and work plans in place, the investors will be able to assess the progress of the business as well as making adjustment that will reduce the risk for the business especially the cash flows risks.

Performance Targets and Reviewing Key Performance Indicators (Focus on Sales, Revenues, Receivables/Payables)

In addition to ensuring that proposer budgets and works plans are in place, it is important that the investor focuses on key performance indicators that will help him or her to assess the success of the business in the achievement of the laid-out budgets and works plans. In this case, the investor will need to focus to about five parameters that should be maintained in a dashboard that will help in assessing the progress and success of the investment. It is necessary to have specific targets for these five indicators and this should be part of the regular reporting from the management of the investee company.

Example of the KPIs could include the following, taking into account that the business is in the nascent stages of growth and cannot be judged fully based on parameters established for mature enterprise:

Sales numbers: This is in terms of units sold, revenues generated from the sales and disaggregation on products and location of sales.

Gross profit margin: As a parameter, profitability helps determine whether money is being made, as well as being a measure of how well the business is doing in terms of managing costs.

Receivables/payables: There is need for the investor keep an eye on both the receivables and payables to ensure that the cash flows and cash cycle are well managed, especially where there is limited funding—it is prudent to avoid calls for additional investments too soon after the initial investment.

Inventory levels: Keeping a keen eye on the inventory levels of a business will also be critical, again to manage the cash flows as well as to ensure that the company has stocks to enable it carry out its mandate without shortages.

Impact measures: In looking to make money, investors should not overlook off the importance of having the business make an impact in its ecosystem.

Too often, the noble goals of impact investing are lost in the clamor for returns.

This parameter will include keeping a tab on the number of employees, the number of customers reached and the number of people whose livelihoods are improving due to the business under consideration. This is a key parameter for impact funds and will take on a different shape and nature for different businesses and for different investors depending on their priorities in terms of impacts.

Investors who feel that these parameters are not being met should not be afraid to cut their losses and exit a business, before the losses overwhelm them. It can also be an indicator that investors should change direction in the way you are running the business—an opportunity to reset goals and operations.

In the case of Bright Chicks, perhaps the investors should have been aware of the problems much earlier and tried to apply remedies, given that the indicators above were all blinking red. First of all, it took the business over three years to break even. In effect, this was three years late, as going by the expectations from the financial projections used to analyze the investment, the business was to get to the break-even level within the first year of operations. In these three years, the business had expanded from Uganda to markets in South Sudan and Burundi.

More than 40% of the total sales of the business was from the export market, something that had not been foreseen in the initial projections.

They also sold the bulk of their poultry products on credit on an average 90-day cycle, which was another deviation from the projection.

The proprietors had instead projected that the business would be able to convert sales into cash within 30 days, and hence, as a result of the longer credit cycle, the cash flow requirement for the business was strained, which did not help to make the investment a success. Most of the export market was also selling in foreign currency, which made the company suffer a foreign exchange risk as the currencies were fluctuating significantly, a very real risk in the case of many African countries.

The market for the products was mainly to big buyers and not to individual customers. The customers for the poultry meat products included hotels, restaurants and supermarkets. In spite of these challenges, the business recorded reasonable success until 2012, when the business came face to face with two major challenges.

First, the second largest cash market for the company, South Sudan, was effectively crippled overnight due to the closure of the border as results of conflict with Uganda. This had a substantial impact in the cash flow of the business. The second challenge was in the local market, where a local rival imported at least 300 tonnes of frozen poultry meat from Brazil.

This had a significant hit on sales of Bright Chicks, which in return resulted in reduced cash flow to the business. The main promoter of the business has been injecting cash into the business to make it move ahead despite the challenges highlighted above. However, it got to a point where the promoters could not inject more money due to unavailability of the same.

The deep pocket element of the impact investing is critical, especially in the cases where the business is faced with cash flow challenges. It is therefore important for the impact investors to keep an eye on the parameters that always give an indicator when things are going wrong.

In the case of Bright Chicks, faced with lack of further funding, the investors and the promoters agreed to put the business up for sale. In the meantime, production was stopped, and the business was no longer an ongoing concern.

Funds Use Restrictions

When a business is making a proposal for investment, it is required that the management of the business provides the required use of these funds. This is important for the impact investor for two main reasons. First, it helps the investor to determine if the investment is worthwhile and if they should be involved. Depending on the investors, there are restrictions on the sort of investment that they can back and on those they cannot. Normally, there is an exclusion list that is maintained by funds; for instance, some restrictions are put on refinancing an existing loan, investment in environmental destructive equipment, investment in non-essentials in the business such as management cars and office furnishing and so on.

The second reason that the funds use detail is important is that it helps the investor determine if their money is being put to the right use. The investor will be tracking and requesting evidence that the funds have been put to proper use as per the plan.

Funding Instrument

The funding instrument that the investor will use to invest in the potential business is crucial for the success of the investment, and its choice can either lower or raise the risk of failure depending on the jurisdiction and the prevailing economic conditions.

The choice of instrument is determined by a number of factors such as the stage of the business, the current and potential cash flows of the business, exit dynamics, mechanisms and overall goal of the investor, and the investment thesis of the investor. The two key instruments normally deployed by investors are debt and equity, although in between there are many variations of the two classes such as preference shares, convertible debts and so on.

In most cases, considering that the impact businesses has a potential in the future, as well as the fact that their cash flows are low and risks high, most investors in the impact space prefer 'equity type' investment instruments. These kinds of instruments are very helpful for the investee companies as they enable the business to be propelled to the next level without much pressure on its cash flow, as would be the case for debt-like instruments.

When the investor takes an 'equity like' position, it means that s/he takes the responsibility to grow the business, which in most cases will be an early-stage start-up and early-stage business, to the next level and hence it is important to align the founders/shareholders of the business with the fiduciary duty in order to improve and scale the business. The investor will henceforth be perceived to be a business and financing partner and therefore over and above the supply of money in the form of the investment, it is expected that the investor will add value to the businesses.

This can be through various means, which will include sitting on the board of the company, taking an active role in the day to day running for the business, which is normally done through the use of the TA money as well as opening doors and networking the businesses for the purposes of value creations.

These activities are not common in traditional investment models and this is because, the assumptions for traditional businesses is that they are mature enough to get to the next level and the role of the investors is supervision through board representation as well as through formal reporting. For the impact financing model, this does not work as the businesses requires substantial hand-holding and investors should understand that the successful cases of impact investment have required a lot of hand-holding and heavy touch TA.

Straight equity investments have a number of challenges that include valuation, where the agreement on the valuation of the social enterprises is a huge point of contention as most social entrepreneurs will always value their businesses at a much higher value than the fundamentals dictates, which results in a lot of walking away by investors.

Exiting the business is another challenge that the investors will face when they invest in straight equity. There have not been many equity investments exist in Africa and this is a reality that impact inventors should be wise to.

The challenge is that African stock markets are not very developed and hence are not part of the exit mechanisms. On the other hand, most of the social enterprises are in growth phase and trade sales will not be options for exits as most of the follow-on investors will insist that the cash/investments they make should be used to grow the business as opposed to paying the investors.

Shareholder terms and agreement complexities is another reason that straight equity is not a very attractive option. Most of the social enterprises do not have mature governance systems and hence the investors will not be guaranteed of the safety of the investments.

As the business scales and additional financing is required, more and more investors will join the bandwagon and probably with more money than the initial investors, hence leading to dilution of the initial investors. In this case, the initial investors will not have much say in the running of the business, which might be against the investment thesis of the impact fund. This could be avoided by having limited or no straight equity instrument.

The most popular instrument that we have seen being deployed in Africa is a convertible debt instrument. This will not pay interest in the first couple of years depending on the cash flow of the business. It means that the funds that would have gone into interest payment will be capitalized over the grace period, which opens up a possibility of conversion after an agreed event. The event will take different shapes depending on each business. This could be the acquisition by another company at a certain level of sales and cash flows and so on.

Since the conversion is an option available to the investor, there is a possibility that the investor may opt out of conversion, which means that the investment instruments will remain as a debt instrument, which will be self-liquidating and hence will not represent a challenge with the exit. It also resolves the challenges of a trade sale where the investors will not be willing to refinance the business.

Given the investment is debt in the balance sheet of the social enterprises, the businesses has the responsibility to repay the debt and hence the investors or the business will be compelled to pay out the loan. The disadvantage of the convertible debt and especially where it is not converted is that it does not provide a benefit to the investors. Although the key objective of impact funds is not to make huge financial return, a reasonable return will be in order for the sustainability of impact funds.

It is possible at the investment analysis and investment commitment for the investor to draw up clauses that will enable the investor to share in the upside in case the instrument is not converted.

Summary

The question, and problem, of risk will always arise. A risk-free investment is probably not going to offer much in return, given the inverse correlation between the two.

The reason I chose to dwell at length on risk and how to mitigate it is due to the real life examples of failure that I have seen in the industry in Africa over the course of my career, arising out of investors ignoring the risk indicators in their chosen line of investment.

We have seen the example of Bright Chicks, a business that could have ticked so many boxes as far as impact on society is concerned. This is a business that would have addressed problems of joblessness across a whole value chain and food security, but it instead went belly-up due to oversight of some obvious and not-so-obvious pitfalls.

What I have learnt from my experience is that risk will never quite go away in totality from a business. As one problem is addressed, another could be on the way, and given that risks are embedded in real life situations that can sometimes be impossible to avoid, the ability to identify the problems early and to take measures to minimise their negative effect is certainly a good skill to have.

One of the most critical measures of risk mitigation that I have seen and one that I enumerated quite early in the chapter, is the investor holding the hand of the investee and using their shared experience to solve any issues that arise. This means that the investor becomes a business partner as opposed to a financing partner, which will also help the investor to keep a better eye on whether the business is making the desired impact in society.

There are a few guiding principles that investors need to have and show in order to help the chances of the business to succeed, which we have listed as being willing to offer TA and tailored finance that suits the investee, be willing to accept to take higher risk than you would normally (i.e. raising your risk tolerance), and also displaying patience with the investee as they try to make their business work.

Before we conclude the chapter, it is also important to emphasize that investors also need to cover themselves and their base against emerging risks associated with investing into someone else's enterprise. Just to list these, investors need to keep an eye on contract terms in order to ensure they not getting a raw deal. In line with this, it is necessary to ensure that the business owner offers some guarantees of his or her own in terms of how much they will invest in resources and time into the business. They also need to agree to a set of performance targets for the business—which will in effect protect investment.

Finally, it will be necessary to do proper market research and proper selection of the funding instrument. With all these in place, the investor will definitely be in a better position to face the emerging challenges that can hit a business, as we shall see in the next chapter of this book.

9

Challenges for Impact Businesses in Africa

Although there has been substantial growth in the impact investing sector in Africa, there are still hindrances to even better growth. There are a myriad of challenges that the sector, investors and investee companies need to deal with.

The discussion in this chapter will be structured into three subsections or dimensions, namely challenges facing the investee companies, those that affect the investors, and challenges to the eco-system. We shall also infuse ideas on how to mitigate some of these challenges, building on some of the ideas we had proposed in Chapter 2 on how to do business in Africa.

Challenges Facing Investee Companies

Business are often faced with the challenge of a lack of business management skills within the management team. This will result in non-optimized results for the business as compared with a situation where the management of the business has the required skills to manage the businesses.

The effect of this is poor business strategies, such as financing, marketing and distribution, and production strategies that will have effect on the level of impacts as well as the financial returns that the business can be able to deliver. This has created a need for business advisory services that could be provided to firms to upgrade their management knowhow in managing their business. This is an even bigger challenge for impact businesses as the founders of these businesses are not necessarily business people and hence have limited skills.

© The Author(s) 2018
E. Mungai, *Impact Investing in Africa*,
https://doi.org/10.1007/978-3-030-00428-6_9

The impact investors will therefore be required to carry out an assessment of the skills gap within the management team before the investment is made. In most cases, the gap in the knowledge is bridged by having technical assistance (TA) money within the investment, which will help the management of the company to upgrade their skills.

In the long-form table, we shall break down the broad dimensions through which this TA can be deployed by investors from a strategic, technical and personnel point of view (Table 9.1).

Access to Finance

Access to finance is another challenge that is faced by the impact investee companies or the social enterprises. This is mainly because the companies will, in most cases, be unable to qualify for or attract the traditional financing, which tends to favor established firms with a proven track record.

Banks, for instance, would be looking to finance companies that carry low risk and have a guaranteed financial return pipeline. They often demand a history of about three years to be able to fund the business. The traditional banking model in regard to provision for credit has not changed in the African continent for the last 20 years. The loan application for individuals as well as the business are still the same forms that were used 20 years ago, despite the innovation and changes that have happened in the last two decades.

This therefore means that the investee companies will not be attractive for this traditional financing, which has resulted in the financing gap that—in what can be described as a silver lining— has opened the doors for impact investors.

However, even though impact investing is one way of managing the gap in financing, it is still not sufficient. There is clearly a need for more innovative financing mechanisms for these businesses that will recognize the stage at which the business is operating, as well as consider sector-specific issues, including consideration of the impact returns as opposed to financial returns.

The financing instruments being used in the sector are also a challenge, mainly due to the lack of innovation. Currently, most of the financing available is plain vanilla financial instruments such as straight debt or equity, which does not work for most impact investing businesses.

There is need to consider other equity-like or debt-like investment instruments as they are more flexible for the business and will not put pressure of the business cash flows, which will help in the achievement of both the financial as well as the impact returns to the investors.

Table 9.1 Technical assistance dimension for impact businesses

Dimension	Support service	Description and venture benefits
Market	Market segmentation and prioritization	Here, it is necessary for investors to help the investee company identify and understand market segments and characteristics of each segment including different customer needs, potential routes to market, and recommended segment prioritization for the venture
	Competitor analysis	Identify competing technologies and businesses delivering those solutions, and then compare the benefits of those solutions with the venture's solution
	Industrial partnering	Identify potential industrial partners, introduce the investee firm to partners, support development of presentations, and advice on negotiations with partner
	Market research	Engage with range of stakeholders across the value chain to understand customer needs and the benefits of the solution the venture is developing
	Market collateral	Support development of introductory material about the venture including introductory presentations, case studies, and websites
Strategy and planning	Having a good market entry strategy	Investors should prioritize the most promising bridgehead market for initial sales
		Highlight potential routes to market in that initial segment and recommend the most promising route (e.g., own manufacture, licensing, joint development, direct sales or distribution) identify key milestones for implementing that route to market
	Business plan	Assist the investee to develop and refine a business plan that will include key milestones for the venture other essential components the business needs to make its venture a success
	Business model	Identify different business model options for the venture and highlight to the investee the advantages/disadvantages of each option

(continued)

Table 9.1 (continued)

Dimension	Support service	Description and venture benefits
Business development and sales	Customer value proposition	Support the venture to develop a compelling story of how the benefits of its solution translate into value for potential customers
	Pipeline development and analysis	Collaborate with the venture to build a pipeline of potential customers and prioritize which customers to focus initial sales efforts on
	Strategic sales	Help to identify and secure the venture's first strategic sale (e.g., the first demonstration client that can act as a reference for future sales)
	Sales analysis	Engage with customers to get feedback on the strengths and weaknesses of the venture's sales approach
Setting up a winning team	Mentoring/coaching	Use wider experience, offer strategic implementation support to CEO and senior leadership team, acting as an independent sounding board on company strategy and growth
	Alignment and communication	Facilitate alignment of the team around a critical issue that needs to be addressed to enable successful commercialization (e.g., market prioritization, fundraising requirements and plans)
	Team development review and plan	Review key competencies within the team, identify gaps that need to be filled to enable the company to grow, support development of plan to address these team gaps and secure priority hire(s)
Board	Board development	Identify strengths and potential gaps on venture's board, advise on and support development of board if none exists, assist in sourcing and selecting appropriate non-executive directors with the expertise and networks to enable the venture to grow
Technology and intellectual property	Technology roadmap	Collaborate with the investee to do an analysis of the venture's current development stage and options for future development, and priority technology development milestones and plans
	Intellectual property	Review the venture's patents to identify strengths and potential gaps that competitors could exploit, freedom to operate searches, support development of IP strategy
	Independent technology validation	Review and validate technology from independent experts to increase potential customer, partner and investor confidence in the solution

(continued)

Table 9.1 (continued)

Dimension	Support service	Description and venture benefits
Product development	Analyze product competitiveness	Compare product functions, features and benefits, and cost/price data with those offered by competitors to identify unique selling points and differentiation
	Design for manufacture	Advise the investee on developing product designs for manufacture, roll out and human interaction
	Product development review	Review prototype demonstration plans and/or plans for first product launch to ensure prototypes/products are sufficient to demonstrate key benefits but are not over-specified. Identify and prioritize key product development steps for future product versions
Supply chain and operations	Supply chain development	Review potential supply chain gaps/risks for the venture, identifying alternative suppliers and qualifying those suppliers where required for manufacturing, key components, assembly, installation and distribution
Funding and administration	Investment readiness	Analysis of fundraising pitch and strategy, develop pitch and strategy (e.g., funding amount, target investors) to create a compelling investment proposition
	Funding sources	Advise on public and private funding sources that the venture has not already pursued, including international funding sources in addition to local funding, and support to pursue these funding sources
	Licensing advice	Advise on licensing terms, introducing the venture to potential licensees, support on licensing negotiations
	Project management	Support the venture to create/develop risk register, project planning tools, development of financial management and procurement processes
	Financial management	Provide advice to improve basic financial management, including budgeting principles, recording and reporting of business accounts. Provide support in selecting external financial/accounting service providers

For the financing to work for the impact business, it requires it to be combined with TA. This point is emphasized here and elsewhere in the book because it is important for impact business as well as investors to understand that capital is a necessary requirement for the business success but not in itself a sufficient requirement due to the challenges highlighted above in relation to the lack of business knowledge for impact business founders.

This means that financing needs to come hand in hand with TA for the business in order to be able to unlock the value and at the same time deliver substantial impacts.

One possibility of growing an impact business is through the investment of the internally generated funds—mainly the retained earnings. This will require the business to grow organically, even though it is a slower growth option, which normally takes a number of years for the business to get to scale. This is the reason that most of the impact businesses will look for external financing that will help them to leverage on their capabilities and hence scale faster. Impact investors will serve as a major source of funding through innovative and non-plain vanilla financing instruments. Other investors will include the traditional private equity funds, foundations and Development Financial Institution (DFIs) depending on the investment ticket size, the sector, the potential for impact and the investing thesis of the investor.

The challenge with getting financing from outside of the impact investors' space is that the instruments as well as the terms of investment are normally not creative or innovative enough to be in line with the needs of the investee companies.

Most traditional investors will restrict themselves to the traditional instruments such as debt and equity and term sheets, as noted elsewhere in this book, which, since they are onerous, makes it difficult for the investments to happen.

Innovative financing instruments and terms will go a long way to enabling the financing of the impact businesses in Africa. Equity-like and debt-like instruments will be best, depending on the businesses evaluation of the investment cases, the investors investment thesis as well as the exit mechanisms considerations.

Access to Information

Access to information is critical to the success of any businesses and even more so for the impact businesses. The information will relate to market distribution, production, technology and other information requirements depending on the business and the sector. Ventures need information to assist them in making informed decisions as they execute their strategies.

The information requirements will be satisfied through initiatives and products such as access to databases, working papers, policy briefs, market surveys and the latest journals on the sector and business, as well as the current trends.

These information products are normally not available for most of businesses in Africa and hence a deliberate move towards the provision of this information will help improve the business operations. As we saw in the previous chapter, this is likely to be one of the key trends going forward in the impact investment space, where, thankfully, critical databases are being created as the sector grows.

Impact investors should therefore endeavor to introduce their investees to their networks, and hopefully the businesses will leverage these networks and hence increase the value of the investment and the expected impact.

This access to information component will involve a number of things, key among them being the impact businesses dipping into global knowledge hubs in order to learn about the latest technologies and business models. The businesses need to get up to date with the latest technologies and system standards, testing, and certification, which can only be done through sharing of information databases, best practices and tools on R&D planning and road-mapping.

Performance data and experiences on various technologies and business and prototyping information is also important as a way of tracking growth in this area. Investors need to emphasize knowledge sharing on best practices and tools for economic assessment, policies and programmes, financing, infrastructure development, and business development.

Provision of the market information and the ability to interpret the market data for betterment of the business results is also key. However, even as investors move to address the information gap in the investee firm, it is important that they take care to avoid duplication when sharing information about similar work elsewhere—which runs the risk of making the investee companies aim to duplicate the experiences of the investor in cases where they actually need to come up with innovations aligned with their local circumstances.

Access to Facilities

Impact investors should consider resolving some of the challenges faced by the investee companies that relate to access to facilities.

This will be in the form of provision of physical space, which will provide a conducive working environment and access to high quality and cost-effective testing, prototyping and development laboratories to deliver the technical component of the companies and communication facilities.

Investee companies, in most cases, lack a physical office, especially when they are starting out and it will be a consideration of the impact investors to provide such physical space that could be shared among a number of investee companies. They can also be directed to existing shared office space, such as the technology hubs that are springing up across Africa. In the same space, there could be provision of services, such meeting facilities as well as ICT provisions.

It could be that the space is used for networking purposes, especially where there will be possibilities for synergies between investee companies in the portfolio of the impact investor.

The economies of scale may not allow for such centralization of portfolio companies by one impact fund, but this is a possibility for a partnership among impact funders to come together and establish hubs across Africa as part of strengthening the impact investing ecosystem. Another possibility is the provision of access to common facilities for prototyping and testing, which is normally an expensive affair for impact businesses and a hindrance to the optimization and testing of their products.

Enabling Environment

Impact businesses need a conducive environment in order to succeed.

In most cases, they will be delivering out-of-the-ordinary products and services, which in most cases will be new in the market, and hence may not be achievable using the methods applied to existing products and services.

Globally, innovation is ahead of policy and hence the innovators and in this case impact businesses will come up with solutions that are not envisioned in the policies and regulations. These products are therefore often labelled "disruptive technology and products" when they hit the market, but soon become accepted as the new norm.

If there is an enabling environment that support impact businesses and investments, especially in the form of policies, are non-existent, the impact businesses will be faced with many challenges, including not being able to sell their products. Their owners and impact investors have to consider a facility where they can provide advice based on the learning experience from the impact businesses and entrepreneurs on hurdles to commercialize or scale-up their products and services.

Various mechanisms addressing feedback and ecosystem dialogues should be put in place to help in detecting the policy and regulatory problems that may affect the impact business and to systematically analyze these and provide evidence-based advice to the relevant policy makers and implementers to make these required changes. This process takes time and will require like-minded people to work together.

Consumer's Choice Limited (CCL), a company that seeks to promote the use of clean cooking energy fuels in mid- to low-income urban homes and slums in Kenya, was one of the beneficiaries of improved tax regime as a result of removal of excise duty on bio-ethanol in Kenya in 2015. The company was admitted to Kenya Climate Innovation Center (KCIC) in 2013, with the company's needs listed as policy reform, establishing a custom-made business model, general management and business skills training.

At the time of joining KCIC, the price of ethanol gel fuel was out of reach for their customers, and hence they needed some form of price reduction on low-grade denatured ethanol. In addition to this, the tax regime in Kenya did not make it conducive to process ethanol gel locally.

Through KCIC and other partners' efforts, the Kenya Government removed excise duty on bio-ethanol in 2015. As a result of the improved tax regime, CCL was able to increase its sale of cooking stoves and had reached 15,000 units by July 2016.

The company is now in the process of establishing an ethanol gel processing plant locally. This will enable the company to economically manufacture ethanol and thus make ethanol more affordable to its customers in Kenya.

This example shows that there is a definite need for impact businesses and impact funds to have some level of a working relationship with policy makers and governments to ensure that the policies and standards that are implemented in the country are more favourable to the impact businesses.

The case of CCL is a good illustration of where there are synergies for these groups to work together. The players should work together to produce policy briefs that can be used to highlight the challenges to the associated stakeholders.

Government policymakers have a lot on their plate at the best of times, and would therefore depend on industry stakeholders to point out areas where policy can be changed in order to assist investors who are looking to make a positive impact on society.

There may be a need for the impact funds and other well-wishers from the international arena to help Africa to push through policies by having international think tanks also working on Africa-related matters and assist governments and policymakers on the best practices as well as international experiences that will move the continent toward self-sustenance and poverty eradication.

Apart from the drafting of the policies, there is a need for stakeholders to convene in workshops and committees that will help shape the agenda for a better enabling environment for impact-related businesses. This agenda will include tax issues, regulation issues and sometimes very specific issues such as product quality and mark of standard in various jurisdictions. This will be the role of the like-minded parties and will include the impact business funders, think tanks, international NGOs, UN bodies and so on.

A good example is the effort in Kenya by UNIDO, which in the recent past has engaged the government of Kenya in policy making, especially in regard to energy issues. This includes issues relating to waste-to-energy and clean lighting facilities, for example. UNIDO helped in the development of a strategy on moving rural households from kerosene-based lighting towards clean lighting.

UNIDO participates in the Energy Donor Coordination group in Kenya that is hosted by the Ministry of Energy and basically coordinates all donor programs in the energy sector. This example needs to be copied in other sectors as well as to other countries across Africa. There is also space to work with the Standards Bureaus across Africa to ensure that the products developed by the impact businesses meets the expected standards and, in cases where there are no standards, to see to it that such standards are developed.

A case in point in Kenya is an impact business that is testing the packaging of biogas in bottles for household consumption in order to replace wood fuels as well as liquefied petroleum gas (LPG). The company has managed to package the gas but, at the moment, faces a challenge in selling the products due to the lack of standards on packaged biogas in Kenya.

To avert such situations, again there is a need for impact businesses, investors and other like-minded people and organizations to work together to deliver better standards for impact businesses.

Challenges Facing Investors

It is not just investees who face challenges in the course of rolling out impact investments. While the impact investor comes into the space with a great deal of knowledge, market research and experience, they too face a set of unique challenges, which we shall show in a bit of detail below.

Deal Flow Challenges

Securing investable business in Africa still remains a big challenge for impact investors. There is fierce competition for the best deals, which has resulted in another challenge where impact investors are overpaying to secure the deals. As one would imagine, there are many possible deals in Africa, but the questions is always whether the deals are ready and whether they meet the required criteria for a particular investor.

In most cases, the deal will not meet the expectations and the trend is now for the fund to provide pre-deal TA to enable them to meet the required criteria.

This pre-deal assistance holds a lot of promise for the investor in making the potential impact business eligible for investment.

A good example would be a business has some level of possible impact, but is not sustainable. In such a case, an impact fund would intervene and assist in providing TA in order to make the business case bankable and hence enrich the pipeline for the fund.

It could also be that a venture has a very good business model but has a challenge in establishing the best financing mechanism. In this case, the impact fund or investor will provide for the pre-deal support to figure out the most optimal financing model for the company to enhance both the impacts from the business as well as the financial return for the fund and the shareholders.

The lack of investor-ready impact businesses is not just an African problem but also a general problem in other markets, mainly because many social entrepreneurs are not built the same as business people and hence the structuring of companies and the business and financing models are normally messy before professional investors come on board.

The mess will sometimes keep away the investors, but if the investor understands the space well, they will be able to mitigate this by providing pre-deal TA that will enhance the chances for the success of the business as well as the level of impacts and expectations of financial returns s from the business in question.

Many investors are also passing up good investment opportunities due to lack of skills for identifying good businesses. Most of the investors are hiring investment bankers and traditional investor advisors to be in charge of deal development, which has resulted in a mismatch in what they think is investable business and what impact businesses are all about.

A good way to identify the mismatch is to look at the formation request lists requested by the investors at the due diligence stage. In my view, these lists are erroneous and are causing havoc to the social entrepreneurs.

What is important in the sector and for the investment is to understand the business model, the team behind the idea, the market for the product and the associated impacts and their scalability. The rest of the considerations are good to have but are not necessary conditions for investment. The impact investor, once they have established that the above are conditions are acceptable, should move in and where some of the things are not in place, should probably consider pre-deal assistance.

From my experience, I have seen that details, such as asking for audited accounts (sometimes by the big four), asking about the lawyers, organization charts and so on, will not help the case.

Difficulties in Measuring Impact, and Lack of Supporting Framework

This issue of difficulties in measuring impacts is well articulated in the chapter on impact measurement. There are difficulties in measuring impact within the impact investment sector since there is no common language for impact measurement.

There have been some global mechanisms established to help resolve this challenge but, unfortunately, several of them are under development that are using different methodologies and definitions. There is need, therefore, for universal and understandable measuring mechanisms.

Whether this will be arriving in the near future is still debatable but there is clear evidence that it is needed if the impact businesses and their investors are to measure the impacts in a uniform way across continents and across businesses. Such initiatives include the IRIS and the Global Impact Investing Rating System (GIIRS). In other cases, investors are developing their own parameters and measurement methods for impacts.

This can as well contribute to the challenges notes above for the pipeline generation since there is no proper way to ensure the baseline and to help the investor to determine whether to invest in a given business. This lack of standardization causes a lot of problems when one is trying to compare impact and sometimes the financial impact of the businesses invested in by the impact investors.

In short, there is great diversity between investors and the social entrepreneurs and their proposed measurement standards. This challenge is complicated by the fact that there is a great diversity among investors' preferences and priorities, as well as among the scope and activities of impact businesses.

Due to the lack of consistent ways of measuring impact, the growth of the sector is restricted. If there was a good framework, it may be the case that the amount of investment in the sector in Africa would be significant. In my view, the SDGs could be used as the framework for this measurement. The lack of such as framework makes communication, transparency between the businesses, the investors, the governments as well as other stakeholders difficult.

The framework should offer performance indicators to guide the impact investors and impact business to track and report their impacts. Even as we develop a universal way of measuring and reporting impacts, we must consider that these businesses are different and hence there should be some level of flexibility in the frameworks.

Limited Innovative Fund and Deal Structures

Impact businesses promise both financial and impact returns, but at the same time they have proved to have a higher risk and hence this perceived risk has kept investors at bay. I contend therefore that more innovative fund structures as well as investment structures are needed that will enable the investors to manage the risks.

Most of the funds participating in the impact sector in Africa are either new or lack the prerequisite experiences, which does not help in terms of mitigating the risks associated with impact investing. One solution to the problem is where different financing mechanisms—'blended financing'—can be used to de-risk some of the investment.

One of the trends that is becoming more common is to use public funds to de-risk investments for the private sector in order to attract such investments. DFID and the Danish Government are playing a big role in the sector in Africa by providing various instruments that help to de-risk investments. This mechanism of giving the firms grants, entrepreneurship challenges, 'first loss' guarantees and risk-sharing mechanisms are all aimed at inviting the private sector to the impact space.

The catalytic funds are also used where different organisations are investing or granting accelerators and incubators with the aim of preparing the business for investments as well as reducing the risk for later stage investors. Private investors also need to consider instruments outside of plain vanilla investment instruments if they are keen to be involved in impact investing. This will take the shape of equity-like or debt-like instruments.

The changes happening in the deal structuring and investment structuring are mind blowing, with new structures emerging that provide the best fit for the investors as well as the social enterprises. The investors as well as investee companies need to keep track of the changes and the new developments in the impact investing space in Africa. This includes addressing some of the challenges that are faced by the impact investors, such as the pipeline issues as well as exits.

Challenges in Exiting Investments

Exits from an investment still stands as a challenge due to lack of development of the financial markets in the sub-Saharan Africa region. This means that the exit options are restricted, and the most viable exit mechanism is trade sales and this does not happen regularly, hence limiting the impact investments in the continent.

Trade sale is where the business is sold to a strategic buyer through outright buying, mergers and acquisitions or in instances where the social entrepreneur buys the business from the investor. Buy-back by the entrepreneur is becoming popular as one of the exit mechanisms, and in most cases the price of the transaction is predetermined at the investment stage.

The stock markets, for instance, are not a very attractive option, with some of the leading markets (Nigeria and Kenya) having very few listed companies compared with the developed world markets. This means that initial public offerings (IPOs) are not an option for the exits from impact investments in Africa as they are in the developed world.

In future, it is hoped that the stock markets will develop and provide options for exits. Presently though, most stocks markets are more inclined toward financial returns and hence there is still an uncertainty with regard to how the stock markets will react to the impact businesses.

Due to the nature of the markets and the focus on the financial returns, it will be critical for the investors as well as social entrepreneurs to consider the implications of looking at stock market exits and to ensure that their impact goals are still intact since the focus on the stock market may lead to mission drift from impact returns to financial returns.

There are also various barriers to listing, which includes the costs of listing being too high, the requirements in terms of governance and reporting, as well as other costs involved in listing such as the advisory services. As such, there is a need for alternative exit mechanisms that are tailor-made for the impacts space.

Valuation determination for the exits is a real challenge since they are not based on market dynamics, which sometimes leads to overpayment or underpayment by potential investors. To mitigate the risk of exits, many impact investors consider self-liquidating instruments as a way of investing, mainly taking debt-like instruments that they will self-liquate a couple of years after the investments.

This has a double-edged sword effect in that it is sometimes not appropriate for the investee companies since it puts strain on the cash flows and at the same time does not provide the investors with the potential for the upside, which is typical for equity-like investments.

In this case, the investors forgo the upside due to the exit limitations. There have also been some discussions of a possibility of developing a social impact stock market in Africa that will be able to provide an alternative exit mechanism. However, this is still years away and therefore may not be a solution to those investing now.

Economies of scale exist in the sense that there are many impact businesses in Africa and hence the idea of establishing a social impact stock market is feasible. There is need to have eco-system supporters contributing to the formation of such a stock exchange, which will help to eliminate one of the major challenges faced by impact investors in the continent.

Challenges for the Sector Ecosystem

Unclear and Inconsistent Enabling Environment

Africa is lacking an enabling environment for businesses that are supporting impact. This is in the form of macroeconomic factors, regulatory and standards issues, lack of financing mechanisms such as an angel network, and the ease of doing business.

This has cut the odds of success for business compared with other jurisdictions—like the West—where the ecosystems are mature and have deliberate ways of supporting businesses to succeed.

There is need for the governments of Africa, the private sector and other stakeholders to look into ways that they can improve the ecosystems from the perspective of an enabling environment in order to enable the impact and social business to be able to scale.

There has also been a challenge relating to the protection of the rights of the investors, which needs to be worked on from the legal perspective in order to guarantee the investors that their investments in these businesses is safeguarded or protected. Other broader matters that need to be worked on include political stability and empowering local financial systems to enable them to support social businesses.

Macroeconomic policy reforms are also necessary, as these form important drivers of investment both in the developing and developed economies. In the recent past, the macroeconomic performance of the continent has been faced with fluctuating inflation and exchange rates, which are all of concern for the investors. However, there is hope that in the coming years the continent will continue to be more stable politically.

The continent has also proved to be fairly insulated from the global shocks; for instance, the financial crisis of 2008, which did not have a significant impact in the economies as it did for the developed countries. However, it is important for an investor to keep track of the situation in Africa since it continues to depend on the developed economies from the West and East, which will mean that future crises in those markets may have a bigger effect on the economic systems of the continent.

It is good to note that over the years there has been some significant improvements in the enabling environment in the continent and this has resulted in more financial flows to the sector in the recent years. The African continent has historically struggled in most of the areas above and this, in the past, has caused constraints for the investors in terms of invest in the continent. This, as noted above, is changing. More flows are now happening and soon the continent will catch up with Asia as a destination for impact investments financing.

To help in improving the enabling environment, it may be necessary to assist in the capacity building of the policymakers in Africa, to ensure that they understand the impact business. Hopefully, as they develop policy intervention, they will have the impact and social enterprises in mind. For instance, when developing tax policies, policymakers may consider incentives for impact businesses.

However, until they become aware of what those businesses represent, it will be difficult for them to put such interventions in place. Lack of such interventions will hamper the investments in the sector across Africa due to the policies implemented by the governments.

Lack of Synergy in the Investing Ecosystems

The impact investment sector in Africa is fragmented, with players pulling in different directions. The impact sector in Africa has not been able to realize any possible synergies that could arise from the well-coordinated sector through the ecosystem players. For instance, there are no proper connectors between those with the deals and those looking invest in the deals. This is something that the continent can borrow from Asia and other markets where the ecosystems are well developed, with players synergizing and hence improving efficiency in the investment value chain.

To the investors, efficiency will mean that they will be able to get to know which investments are looking for funding and hence will reduce the search cost as well as time. If, for instance, there were databases that could provide details of such investments it would make sense for the investors to subscribe to those databases, which would definitely reduce the costs.

Investing in the sector is also challenging due to the absence of investments support services. However, the situation is improving with more and more practitioners understanding impact investing in the continent. The likes of the investment advisors, advocates, accountants and so on are getting conversant with the sector and services have improved over time, but this still requires more engagement to improve efficiency.

In recent times, there has also been an emergence of networks that are serving the sector. This include the likes of the Aspen Network of Development Entrepreneurs (ANDE) as well as regional and sub-regional networks such as the Southern African Impact Investing Network.

These networks provide advocacy, convening and capacity building roles for the sector. There is also a great role for the government and academia in terms of contributing to the ecosystem of impact investing in the African continent. Academia and government research institutions should come up with initiatives that would facilitate research and development within their campuses as well as building possible businesses that could form part of the pipeline for investment for the impact investors. This will provide opportunities such as those that arose in Silicon Valley, CA, USA in the 1970s and later in Austin, TX, USA.

The 'Austin' and the 'Silicon Valley' models are good starting points for Africa, from which we can take some useful lessons that can be implemented. Hopefully, impact investing will thrive.

Lack of Research and Data on the Impact Sector

Insights on the happenings of the impact investing space are not readily available. In recent times, there has been significant efforts to carry out research on the space. Various foundations, multilaterals, consultancy companies and NGOs have over the last three years been working on different perspectives of impact investing in Africa with the hope of developing a knowledge product able to help investors and the investee to make better decisions as well as better strategies.

This effort must continue in order generate lessons across the continent on investing in impact investing. However, what should be noted is that the markets are still very different and having a one-size-fits-all report for Africa will not make sense. The trend so far is that the research carried out is based in regions such Southern Africa, East Africa and West Africa, which makes a lot of sense.

There is need to add a caveat that, even at the countries level, the dynamics are also different and this needs to be factored in by the consumers of such reports. In closing, let us appreciate that challenges and opportunities are the name of the game for impact investors.

Hopefully, throughout the book I have demonstrated that the impact investing universe in Africa is the way of the future, and a very good solution to the development problems facing the continent. Often, the Africa, continent has been painted with a single brush that spells out problems such as underdeveloped infrastructure, lack of clear rule of law, corruption, uneducated workforce and civil strife. While these issues certainly exist, I hope in this book I have been able to demonstrate that within Africa lies opportunity and a vibrant economy that is offering some of the best returns to investors around the world. It is, in my view, also the place that is most conducive for, and receptive to, impact investment.

Throughout the book, we have dwelt on the theme of impact investments as the way of the future, using vivid examples of successful and not-so-successful cases of investment on the continent to guide the view. This is the place in which an impact investor's capital will have the most visible, and certainly appreciated, effect.

By looking at the risks, challenge and opportunities that the book enumerates, the impact investor will be able to approach a potential opportunity with their eyes wide open, awareness that will help both they and the investee make a success of the venture.

Perhaps more work needs to be done to educate investors on designing funds that are fit for purpose in Africa, where we have seen that the Eurocentric approach may not work due to the unique set of circumstances that the African continent carries. Work also remains to be done in measuring impact, but my belief is that this is an area that will be refined in due course as the experiences of impact investors in Africa deepen.

Overall, we have learned lessons from impact investing in the African continent and should aspire to deploy these in order to improve the space for future investors.

Index

© The Editor(s) (if applicable) and The Author(s) 2018
E. Mungai, *Impact Investing in Africa*,
https://doi.org/10.1007/978-3-030-00428-6

Printed by Printforce, the Netherlands